Sue Rose

# 100 **bright ideas** for
# COLOR

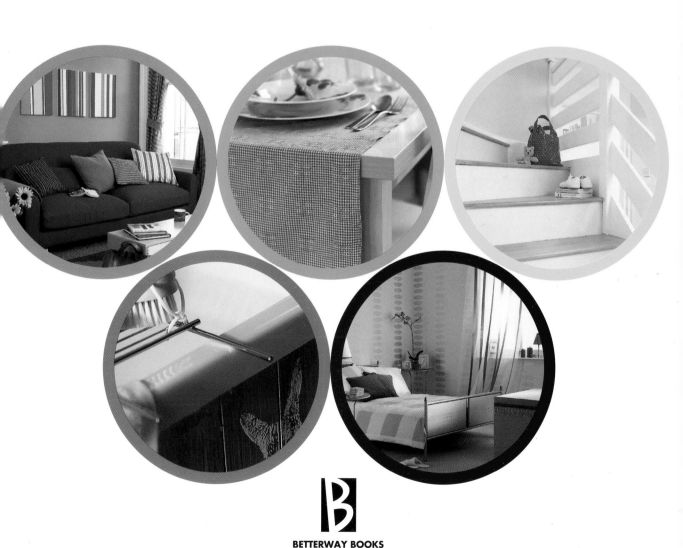

## **BETTERWAY BOOKS**
Cincinnati, Ohio

First published in North America in 2002 by

Betterway Books,

 an imprint of F&W Publications, Inc.,

4700 East Galbraith Road

Cincinnati, OH 45236

1-800-289-0963

ISBN 1 558 70628 3


A CIP catalogue record for this book is available from the British Library


Printed and bound in China


10 9 8 7 6 5 4 3 2 1

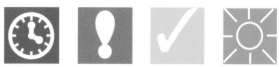

# Contents

# Introduction

No other single element has such an impact on the way your home looks and feels. Colour can make a room feel larger or smaller, bright and airy, cosy, cool or seductive. Colour is far more than simply the shade you decide to put on the wall. Like choosing an outfit to wear, it's the accessories and details that lift a look out of the ordinary. That's why in this book there are hundreds of ideas, tips and projects to bring colour into your home.

## What is colour?

Everything has a colour, so although we tend to think of blue, red or yellow as the kind of colour we might choose to paint a wall, white is just as important in the colour mix. Bear in mind, too, that metal has a colour, as does wood, so the colour of your stripped floorboards is just as vital as those sage green walls.

## How to choose colour

A well-dressed room has layers of colour. The walls and floor are the largest expanses of surface, so choose the colours for them as the basis for your colour scheme. The furniture and window treatments are the next layer of colour. These will usually complement the base colours, often in a stronger shade so that they stand out as focal points in the room. Finally, the accessories – the cushions, rugs, vases and other pictures – add the little touches of contrasting colour that bring a room to life.

## The colour wheel

It's easier to see how colours will work together if you check them on the colour wheel. This places all the colours of the rainbow in a circular spectrum so that you can see at a glance which colours will work well together (those that are opposite each other), which ones will be a sophisticated blend (the shades either side of a colour) and which colours will clash if you don't use them carefully.

## How to put colours together

As a general rule, for a room that is to look pretty or relaxing, choose colours that complement each other. This means they blend well and have a similar intensity of colour. For a more dramatic, lively result, choose colours that contrast, or even clash. As a rule of thumb, try to have no more than four main colours in a room.

## Bright ideas

Each chapter in this book is divided into the following four sections.

 **DONE IN A DAY**

Projects requiring some basic DIY skills that you will be able to complete in a day or less.

 **QUICK FIX**

Instant ideas which are simple to do and will take less than a morning.

 **GOOD IDEAS**

A gallery of inspirations for good buys and finishing touches to make a difference quickly.

 **GET THE LOOK**

Whole decorating schemes for you to recreate and adapt to your own style, with tips on how to achieve the look.

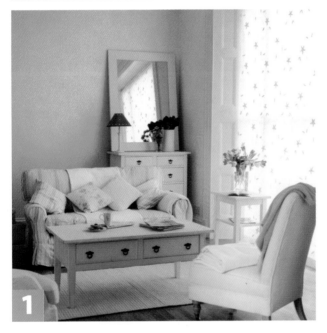

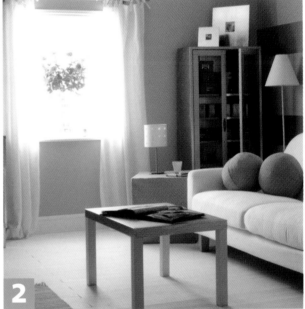

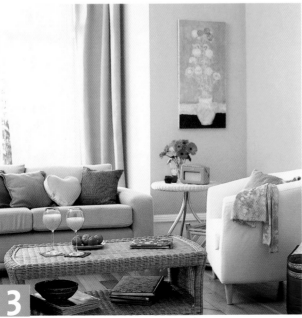

1 **The relaxed look:** Here, yellow and white are the two main colours. Although it looks as though yellow is the dominant colour, there is actually more white in the room, which makes it look very fresh. The green in the fabrics complements the yellow perfectly, while accents of pink, pinky-lilac and lilac stop it all looking too bland. The result is a well-balanced room that looks and feels comfortable.

2 **The formal look:** In contrast to the relaxed living room in yellow and white, this room is very stylized. With just white, green and silver in the room, the look is far more rigid.

3 **The dramatic look:** Colours that contrast, like orange and pink, can look great together if you choose shades that are similar in intensity. The gentle colours of the wood and wicker blend into the background.

# Change the look with colour

The three pictures below show how to achieve dramatically different results in the same room simply by changing the colours of the finishing touches. In each room, the walls are the same blue, with the same off-white sofa and woodwork and the same beech floor. All that has been changed are the window dressing, the cushions and accessories.

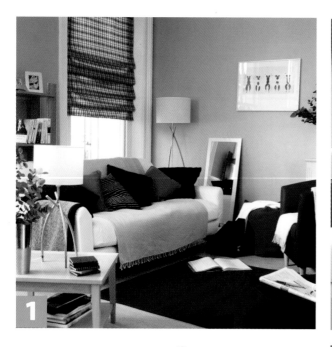

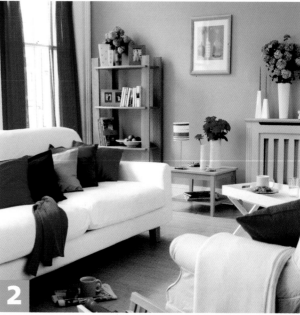

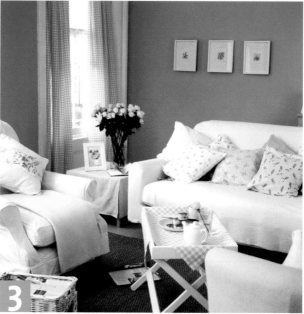

1 Stick to many shades of the same colour for a room that looks smart and sophisticated. Use blues in every shade from baby blue to deepest indigo and you can't go wrong.

2 Pick bright, bold colours and mix and match them to really bring a room to life. These strong, intense shades of pink, lime and blue become the focus of attention in the room.

3 Blue and yellow are opposites on the colour wheel, which means they sit together happily, particularly if you pick soft tones.

## Tips and techniques

Here is a quick-reference guide to some of the materials and do-it-yourself (DIY) techniques involved in the projects in this book.

### MDF

MDF (medium-density fibreboard) is a dense sheet material made from compressed wood fibres. Always wear a dust mask when cutting MDF as the very fine dust is harmful if inhaled over time.

### PRIMER

MDF should always be primed before being painted. This step is similar to undercoating wood and stops too much paint being sucked into the MDF as it is painted. You will generally get a better finish when painting wood if you undercoat first, but it is not necessary if you are painting only small areas. If you are painting untreated pine, first seal any knots in the timber with knotting solution. This will prevent the resin from 'bleeding' through the paint and ensure the paint adheres evenly over the wood.

### PAINT

Being water-based, emulsion paint is easy to use, dries quite quickly and is easily cleaned off paintbrushes. It is particularly suited to painting walls. Oil-based paint provides a tougher, moisture-resistant finish. It can be trickier to apply and dries to either a sheen or a gloss finish.

### VARNISH

To protect a decorative finish, an absorbent surface or a water-based paint such as emulsion, use varnish to provide a hardwearing top coat. You will usually need more than one coat of varnish. In most of the projects in this book, an all-purpose, clear, matt varnish is ideal.

Sometimes you will need a varnish specifically for wood. Acrylic varnish generally gives a matt finish, while polyurethane varnish gives a much harder, shinier result.

### TOOLS

An **electric drill** is an indispensable DIY tool. Most drills come with a set of 'bits' of differing sizes and uses. Match the size of the drill bit to the size of the screw you plan to use. Where you are drilling into a wall, use a masonry bit, which is designed to go through hard surfaces. Insert a wallplug in the drilled hole, then drive the screw into the wallplug. When screwing into wood, the drilled hole should be very slightly smaller than the screw so that the screw grips the wood tightly as it is screwed into place. **Wallplugs** are unnecessary for holding screws in wood.

A **panel saw** is ideal for sawing lengths of wood or MDF. To cut smaller pieces into shape, a **tenon saw** is preferable. A **workbench** with a clamp is useful for making sawing easier.

## Key to symbols used in this book

Check how long the project will take and how easy it is to do with the at-a-glance guide.

  **SKILL LEVEL** Tells you how easy or difficult the project is.

 I DAY

**How LONG** Tells you how long the project will take.

**You will need**
• tape measure
• handsaw
• lengths of 1cm (³⁄₈in) pine board

easy

medium

difficult

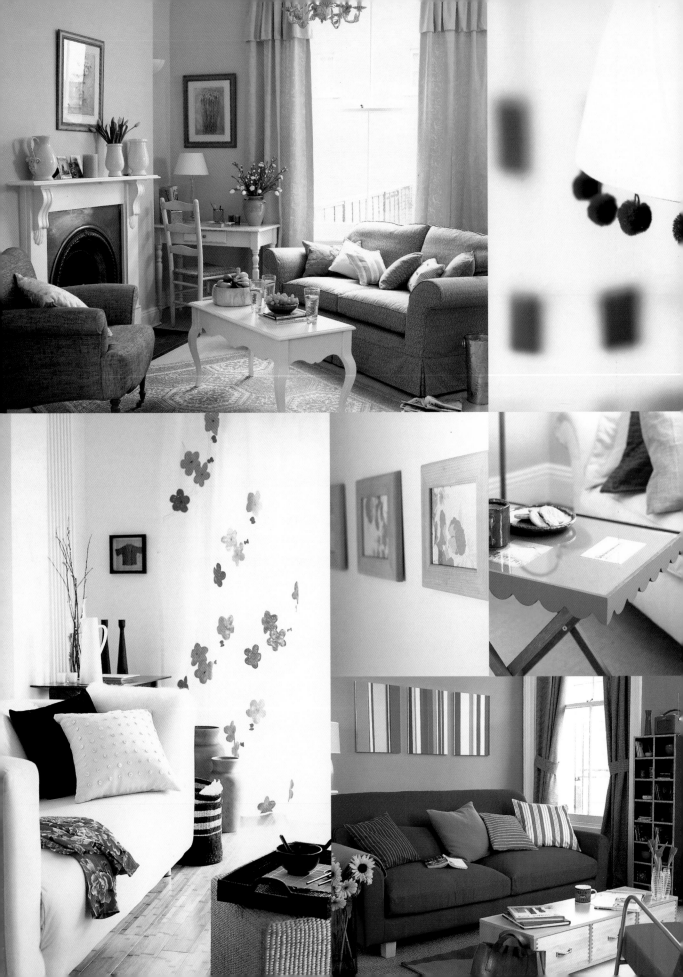

# Living room

The living room is the most public room in the house, used by friends, family and visitors. It is probably also where you spend most of your leisure time, so it needs to be welcoming, comfortable and truly 'you'.

A good colour tip here is to choose easy-to-live-with shades for the largest areas – the floor and the walls – and use stronger colours for window treatments, rugs, cushions and accessories. It is then easy to change items like curtains and cushions if you want to give your living room an update later on.

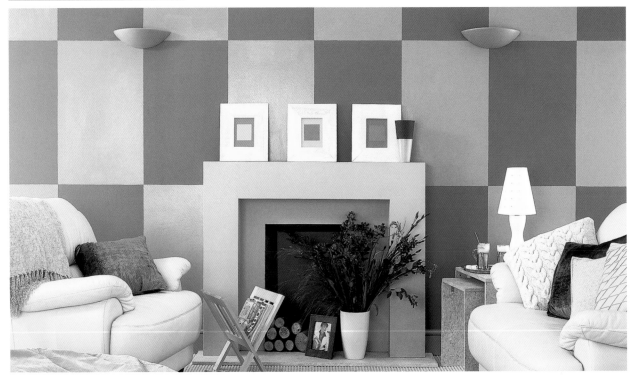

# Chequerboard walls

Transform a plain wall with a painted two-tone effect highlighted with a gloss varnish. Use contrasting colours, different shades of the same colour or just one colour and give alternative squares a gloss finish.

⧗ **4 HOURS**
per wall
plus drying

**You will need**
• emulsion paint in two colours
• household paintbrushes
• tape measure
• spirit level and pencil
• acrylic gloss varnish

**1** Paint one of the colours all over the wall and leave to dry. Measure the wall from skirting to ceiling and from side to side to find the best size of check so as to avoid ending up with small rectangles against doors, windows or fireplaces. Then, using a spirit level and pencil, lightly mark out chequers on the wall.

**2** Fill in alternate sections with the second colour of paint to achieve the chequered effect. Use a smaller paintbrush to mark the edges and

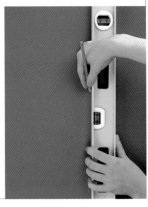

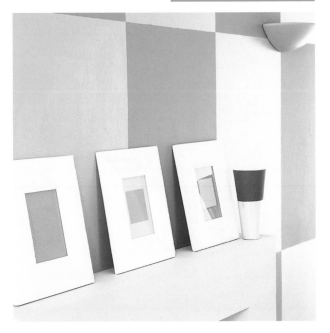

corners of each chequer first, then fill in the main body of the chequer with a bigger brush. To achieve sharp lines around the edges of the chequers, try putting a small elastic band around the base of the paintbrush bristles to stop stray bristles spoiling the outline.

**3** When the second colour is dry, apply acrylic varnish over one of the chequer colours for a shiny effect, again using two sizes of paintbrush as above.

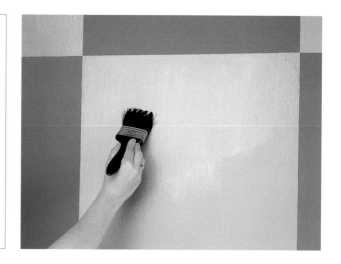

# Revamped side table

This pretty distressed look will work for any wood, or even melamine, furniture, if you apply a suitable primer first.

**1** Make sure the table is clean and dry. Paint it all over with the white emulsion paint, keeping the brushstrokes in one direction. Leave to dry.

**2** Stick masking tape to form a border on the table top, all round the edge,

**2 HOURS** plus drying

### You will need
- square side table, primed if necessary
- emulsion paint in white, plus one other colour
- household paintbrushes
- low-tack masking tape
- tape measure
- quick-drying clear varnish

2cm (¾in) in from the edges. Paint all over the table top with the second colour of paint, using very little paint on the brush so as to achieve a thin coat that shows some of the white underneath. Again, keep the brushstrokes all in one direction.

**3** Leave to dry thoroughly, then remove the masking tape carefully to reveal lines of white around the table top. Finish off the table with a coat of clear varnish to seal and protect it.

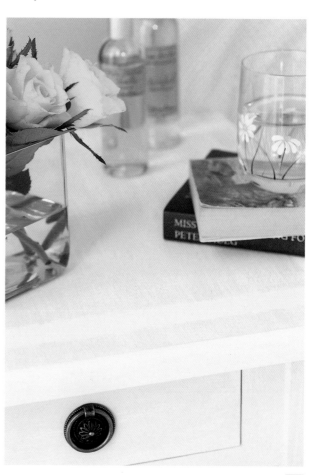

# Raspberry colourwash

Give plain walls texture and depth with this easy colourwashing paint technique. Practise on a sheet of card first until you feel confident to work on the walls.

**2 HOURS**
per wall
plus drying

**You will need**
• vinyl matt emulsion paint in white or cream, plus one other colour such as raspberry
• household paintbrushes
• wallpaper paste
• lint-free cloth

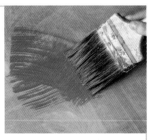

**1** Paint the walls with the white or cream emulsion paint. Leave to dry. Prepare your colourwash by mixing equal parts of wallpaper paste with the other colour of paint. Stir well. Dip a large brush into the colourwash mixture, taking care not to overload the brush. Apply to the wall using random brushstrokes of even pressure.

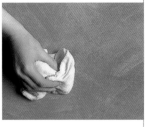

**2** Paint over an area, no more than a metre (yard) wide, from skirting to ceiling, then take the cloth and immediately, and lightly, wipe over the brushstrokes with gentle, sweeping movements to blend in the brush marks. You can leave the brushed effect if you prefer, although using a cloth will smooth any harsh stroke and give a softer, more uniform colourwash.

**3** Repeat, working around the room in sections at a time, working quickly and continuously while the glaze remains workable. Make sure that you blend in the brush marks where you start a new section.

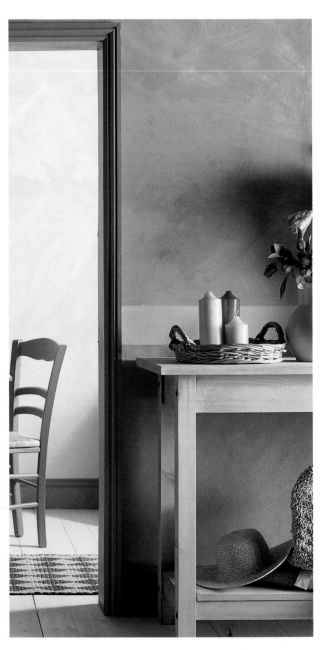

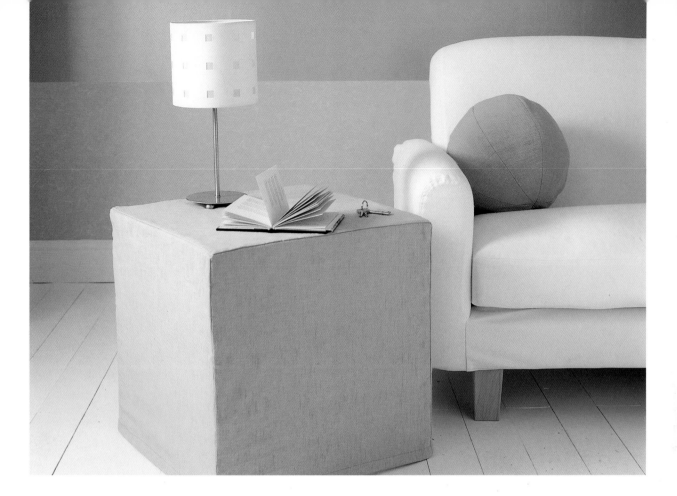

# Fabric cube

Use this wonderfully versatile foam cube as a side table, extra seating or a coffee table. Foam can often be bought and cut to size at local markets.

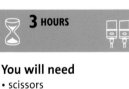

**3 HOURS**

**You will need**
- scissors
- fabric
- tape measure
- dressmaker's pins
- sewing machine or needle and thread
- 50cm (20in) foam cube
- iron

**1** Cut out five squares of fabric, each measuring 54 x 54cm (21½ x 21½in), and lay them out on the floor in a cross shape, the right side of the fabric facing down. Pin each outer square to one edge of the central square, taking a 2cm (¾in) seam allowance.

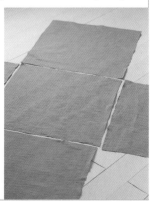

**2** Stitch along the four pinned seams. Pin, then stitch the side seams together to form five sides of a cube, again taking a 2cm (¾in) seam allowance.

Lastly, stitch a 2cm (¾in) hem around the bottom of the cover.

**3** Press the seams, then turn the fabric cover the right side out and slip it over the foam cube.

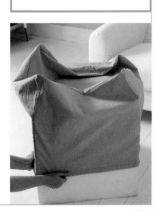

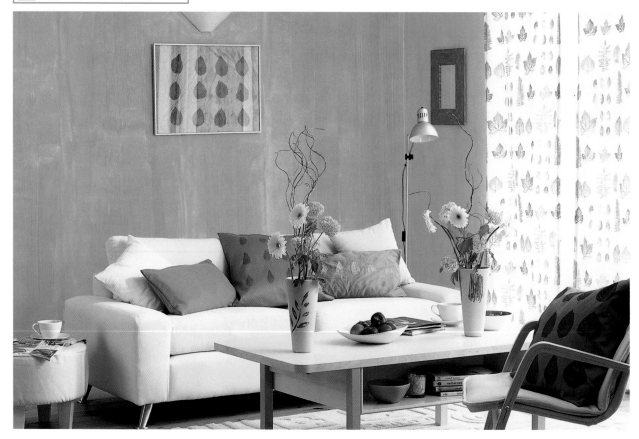

# Dragging effect

One of the easiest paint techniques, dragging creates a subtle, textured effect, which is easy to live with and brings new interest and life to plain walls. It is important to work quickly and to do each wall at one time.

**2 HOURS**
**per wall**
**plus drying**

**You will need**
• vinyl matt emulsion paint in white, plus one other colour
• household paintbrush
• acrylic glaze
• short-pile roller
• dragging brush

**1** Prepare the walls by first painting them with the white emulsion paint. Leave to dry. Make up the colour glaze by mixing one part coloured paint with one part acrylic glaze and three parts water.

**2** Using a short-pile roller, apply the paint glaze to an area of wall about a metre (yard) wide, from skirting to ceiling. Immediately drag the dragging brush over the wet paint from ceiling to floor, using a firm but light touch to leave a dragged effect behind.

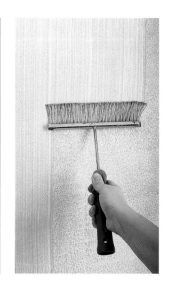

**3** Repeat the process until the entire wall has been dragged, working quickly and continuously while the glaze remains workable.

# Hand-printed cushion

If you cannot find the exact fabric you need for your room, try printing your own. It's simpler than you think and means you can get the exact colour, motif and pattern you need.

**2 HOURS**
plus drying

## You will need
- scissors
- length of plain fabric
- square cushion pad
- tape measure
- fabric paint
- artist's paintbrush
- large sheet of acetate
- dressmaker's pins
- sewing machine or needle and thread
- self-adhesive touch-and-close tape
- iron

**1** Cut out two squares of fabric to fit the cushion pad, allowing 2cm (¾in) extra all round for the hems. Lay the fabric out flat on a firm surface, right side up.

**2** Using fabric paint, paint a leaf shape on to the acetate, then take the wooden end of the brush and scratch out the leaf veins. Dip the wooden end of the brush into the paint to draw on a stalk to finish the leaf. Repeat to create a pattern of leaves.

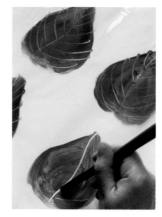

**3** Press the acetate, paint side down, on to the fabric to create your printed image. Lift the acetate carefully to reveal the design.

**4** When the paint is completely dry, pin the fabric squares together, right sides facing. Stitch around three sides of the cushion cover, taking a 2cm (¾in) hem. Press under the raw edges on the open side of the cushion cover. Turn the cover the right side out, insert the cushion pad and finish the opening using the touch-and-close tape cut to length.

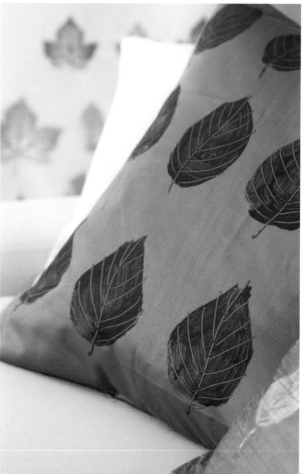

# A touch of autumn

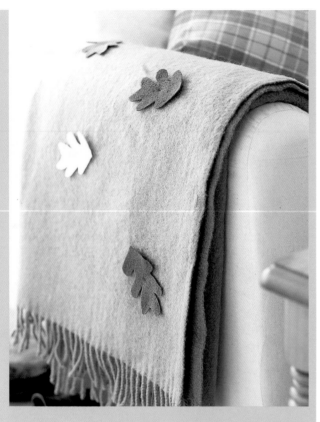

## Autumn leaves lampshade

• Work out the position of your dried leaves on the lampshade before you begin. Place them on the shade, using a thin layer of craft glue to fix them in place. Smooth carefully with a soft cloth.

 **20** MINUTES

**You will need**
• dried leaves (available from craft centres)
• plain lampshade
• craft glue
• soft cloth

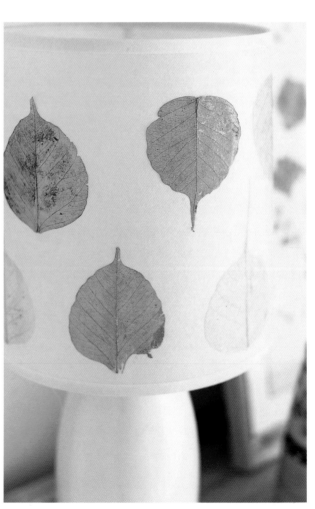

## Felt motifs blanket

• Make a leaf template from card, then use it to cut out different coloured leaf shapes from the felt. Pin the felt leaves on a plain throw or blanket to get an idea of the best arrangement. Handstitch in place to finish.

 **45** MINUTES

**You will need**
• pencil and card
• scissors
• felt in three colours
• plain throw or blanket
• dressmaker's pins
• needle and thread

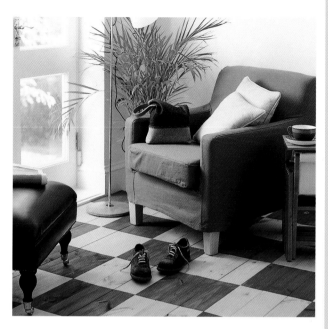

## Chequered woodstain floorboards

● Prepare the floorboards by sanding any protruding edges ensuring they are clean of dust or grease. Using a sponge, stain the boards with the lighter colour woodstain and leave to dry.

● Using a pencil, set square and steel rule, mark out squares on the floor, each

square the width of three floorboards. Score along the edges of the squares with a craft knife to stop the stain bleeding into adjacent squares. Mask off alternate squares using low-tack masking tape, pressing the tape down firmly.

● Carefully sponge the dark stain over the boards to colour alternate squares. When the woodstain is dry, remove the masking tape and apply several coats of quick-drying floor varnish. Leave to dry for at least 24 hours before walking on your new floor.

## Fabric canvases

● Trim the fabric so that it is larger than the artist's canvas by at least 5cm (2in) all round. Lay the fabric right side down on a firm, flat surface and centre the canvas, face down, on top of the fabric.

● Fold one long side of the rectangle of fabric over the side of the canvas and fix to the inside edge of the frame using a staple gun. Repeat with the opposite side, making sure the fabric is pulled taut, but not overstretched, before stapling. Fix the top and bottom edges of the fabric in the same way, folding in the corners of the fabric neatly. Check that the fabric is not overpulled or distorted before the final stapling.

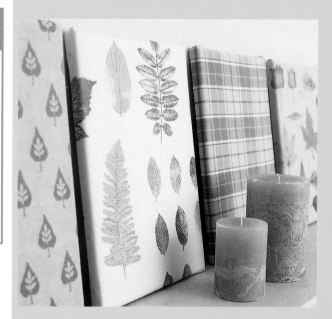

# In the pink

## Feather motifs vase

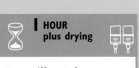

● Cut out the photocopied feather images – you will find it easier to use a craft knife rather than scissors. Stick the images on to the vase using PVA glue. Seal them on to the vase and protect them by giving the whole vase a couple of coats of acrylic varnish. Leave to dry before use.

⌛ **1 HOUR**
**plus drying**

**You will need**
• feather images, colour photocopied to size
• craft knife
• plain ceramic vase
• PVA glue
• acrylic varnish and small brush

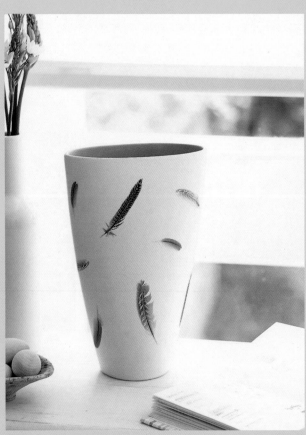

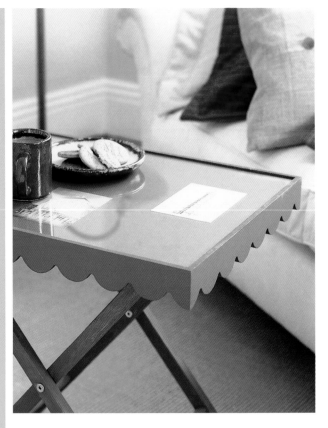

## Photo gallery coffee table

● Arrange photographs or postcards on the table top until you are happy with the positioning. Add a dab of glue to the back of each to stop them moving around. Carefully lay the glass on the table top.

⌛ **30 MINUTES**

**You will need**
• photos or postcards
• small table with recessed top
• PVA glue
• toughened glass, cut to size of table top

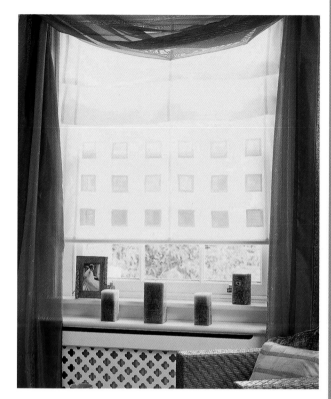

## Custom-made workspace

- Lightly sand, clean and dry the table and chests. Paint the outside of the chests and the drawer fronts with one coat of eggshell paint, leaving to dry between coats. Do not paint the base of the chests. Glue the chests to the top of the console table, lining up with the corners. Leave the glue to set.

**2 HOURS plus drying**

### You will need
- console table in unfinished wood
- wooden mini drawer chests
- sandpaper
- eggshell paint
- household paint brushes
- strong wood glue

- Paint the table and chests all over with eggshell paint. Give the table a second coat. Leave to dry. Look out for simple wooden drawer files and magazine files which you can paint and glue together to make filing storage.

## Voile squares blind

- Draw and cut out two squares from the card, one 2cm (¾in) smaller all round than the other. Lay the larger square on to the iron-on tape and cut out as many squares as you plan to use on your blind. Lay the smaller card square on to the centre of each iron-

**2 HOURS**

### You will need
- ruler, pencil and card
- sharp scissors or craft knife
- iron-on, no-sew tape
- iron
- dressmaker's pencil
- plain blind
- 0.5m (½yd) voile

on tape square and lightly draw around it using a dressmaker's pencil.

- Place the blind, wrong side up, on a flat surface and position the iron-on tape squares on the blind. Iron them in place then carefully cut through both the tape and the blind along the lines of the pencilled smaller squares. Using the larger card template again, cut out squares of voile. Peel away the backing paper from the edges of the iron-on tape squares on the blind and position the voile on top. Iron in place.

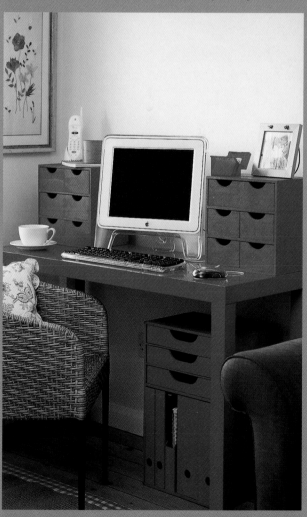

# Splashes of blue

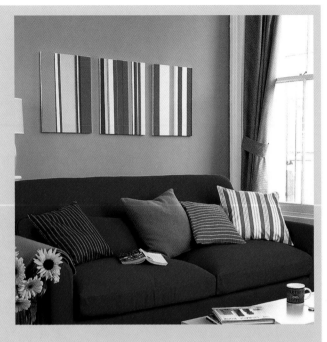

## Button-decorated picture frame

● Take the picture and mount out of the frame and lay the mount flat on a table top. Space out your chosen buttons along the picture edge of the mount until you are happy with the spacing and mix of colour. Working with one button at a time,

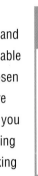

⏳ **10** MINUTES

**You will need**
• picture frame with wide mount
• small flattish buttons of similar size
• PVA glue
• paintbrush

pick up the button and dab a little glue on its underside using a paintbrush. Press on to the mount. Leave the glue to dry thoroughly before reassembling the picture frame.

## Modern art

● Paint the canvas all over with the white emulsion paint. When dry, use a pencil with a spirit level to mark vertical stripes and bands on the canvas in widths varying from 1cm to 4cm (⅜–1½in).

⏳ **2** HOURS **plus drying**

**You will need**
• artist's canvas
• emulsion paint in white, plus various other colours
• assorted brushes, including very fine
• pencil and spirit level
• acrylic varnish

● Paint the bands of lightest colour first, before moving on to the deeper colours, always leaving the stripes to dry between each colour. Finally, use the very fine brush and spirit level to add slim lines of a deep colour, to highlight a pale band or to draw a line of colour through one of the pale bands. Seal the canvas with a coat of varnish to finish.

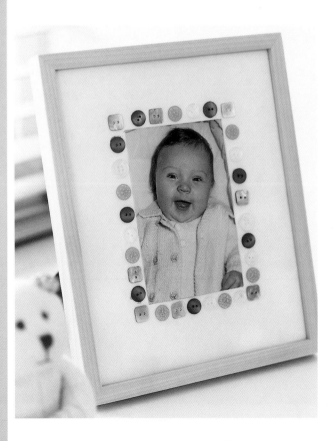

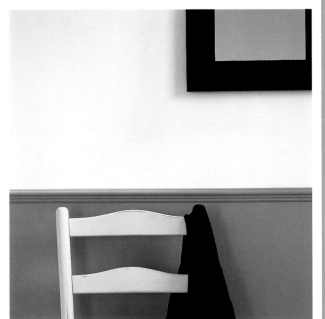

## Adding a dado rail

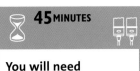

• Measure the width of the wall and cut the dado rail to length using a mitre block. Measure the height you want the rail (usually just above one-third of the way up the wall) and make a small pencil mark. Continue measuring and marking all the way along the wall.

**45 MINUTES**

**You will need**
• tape measure
• dado rail
• handsaw and mitre block
• pencil and spirit level
• hammer and panel pins, or 'liquid nails' glue

• Hold the dado in place and use the spirit level to check that it is horizontal. Using panel pins or 'liquid nails' glue, attach the rail to the wall, putting a pin or blob of glue every 50cm (20in) or so. Paint the rail and the wall below it in a contrasting colour to give extra interest to your living room.

• Lay the blind flat on a table top and place the trim along the bottom of the blind so as to overlap by 1cm (⅜in) at each end. Fold the excess trim over at each end to avoid fraying and pin. Pin the trim all along the edge of the blind. Handstitch in place.

 **I HOUR**

**You will need**
• blind
• tassel trim or fringing, 2cm (¾in) longer than the width of the blind
• tape measure
• dressmaker's pins
• needle and thread

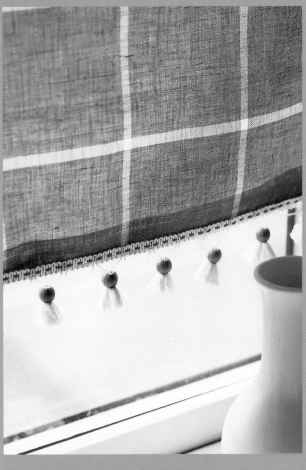

# Detail is everything

## Hand-painted flower curtains

● Draw a simple flower shape on to the card and cut it out to make a template. Place the template on the curtain fabric and draw around it with the fabric pen. Carefully fill in the shape with a paintbrush dipped in fabric dye. Continue working until you have the desired pattern across all the fabric.

⏳ **2 HOURS** plus drying

**You will need**
• pencil and card
• scissors or craft knife
• plain voile curtains
• fabric pen
• artist's paintbrush
• liquid fabric dye

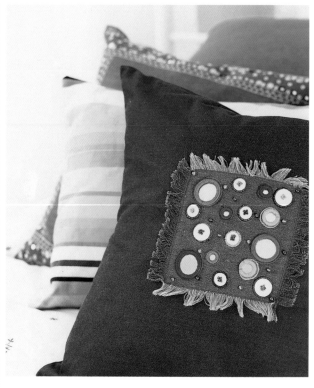

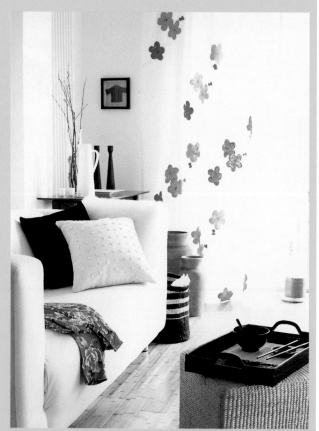

## Decorative cushions

● Remove the cushion pad from its cover. Cut denim into a square to fit in the centre of the cushion. Fray edges heavily to create a fringe. Stitch appliqué motif on to the denim square using embroidery thread. Dot french knots of embroidery thread around between the motifs. Hand stitch square on to cushion cover.

⏳ **30 MINUTES**

**You will need**
• plain cushion with removable cover
• needle and thread
• scissors
• dressmaker's pins
• denim fabric
• appliqué motifs from haberdashery store
• embroidery thread

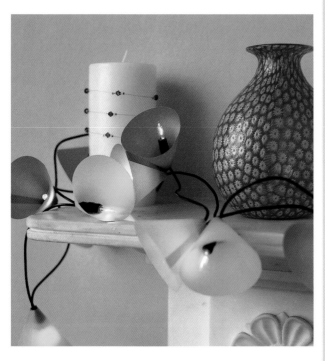

## Bobble trim lampshade

● Measure around the inner bottom edge of the lampshade and cut the bobble trim to length. Apply glue just inside the bottom edge of the lampshade and press on the trim. Hold in place for a few seconds, then continue working around the edge, sticking down a little of the trim at a time. When the entire rim is covered, snip off any excess trim and glue it so that the edges join neatly.

**20 MINUTES**

**You will need**
- tape measure
- plain lampshade
- scissors
- bobble trim
- all-purpose glue or hot-glue gun

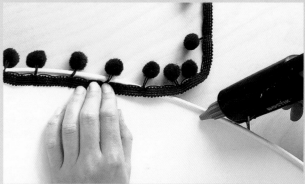

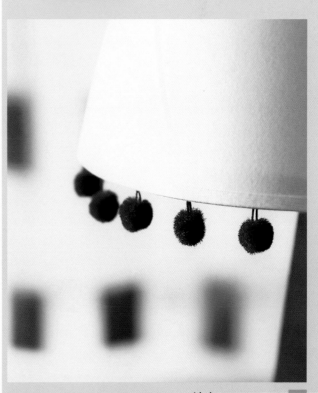

## Coloured string of lights

● Treat the sheets of paper with fire-retardant spray according to manufacturer's instructions. Using a compass and a pencil, mark 15cm (6in) diameter circles on the paper. Each circle will provide a shade for two lights.

**2 HOURS**

**You will need**
- heavyweight semi-transparent paper in a selection of colours
- fire-retardant spray
- compass, ruler and pencil
- scissors
- string of fairy lights
- double-sided sticky tape

● Cut out the circles, fold them in half and cut 1cm (⅜in) diameter circles from the centre of each. Then cut each paper circle in half. Cut 6.5cm (2⅝in) lengths of sticky tape and apply a piece of tape to the straight edge of each semi-circle. Wrap a semi-circle of paper around each bulb and stick the edges together, making sure the bulb doesn't touch the paper.

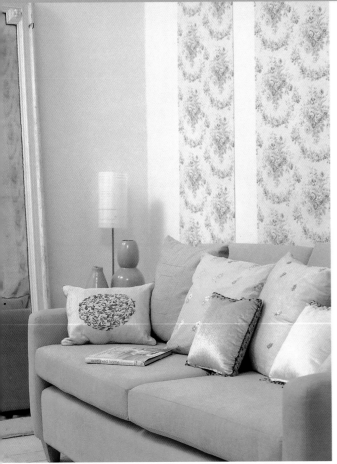

▲ Using strips of highly decorative wallpaper as panels is very effective and not as overpowering as papering a whole room.

# Sugared almonds

For a soft look, pretty up your room with the colours of sugared almonds. Choose pastel-coloured paints and wallpapers, cushions and other accessories.

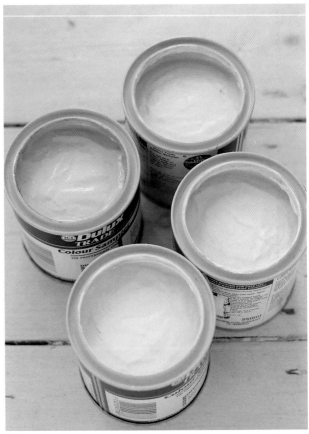

▲ Pastel colours mix together beautifully – try teaming lilac with sugar pink, aqua and baby blue.

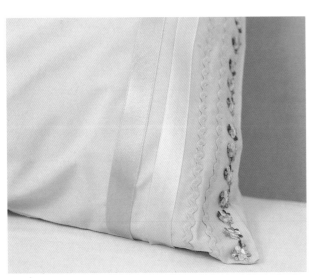

▲ Make an inexpensive cushion into something special by adding a beautiful trim. Try ribbons of velvet, lace or satin, or stitch on strips of fabric as a border.

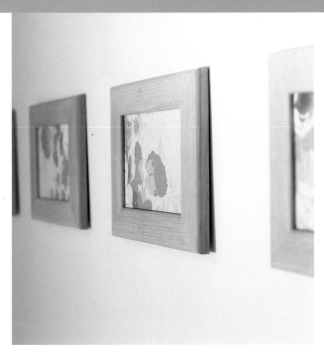

▲ Put offcuts of wallpaper or fabric into picture frames and hang them in a row on the wall.

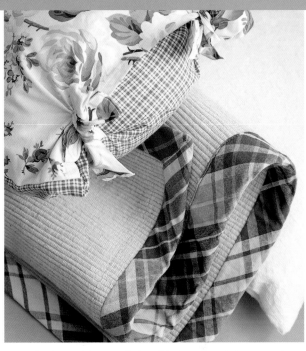

▲ Make a plain rug tie in with the rest of the room by trimming it with leftover curtain or cushion fabric.

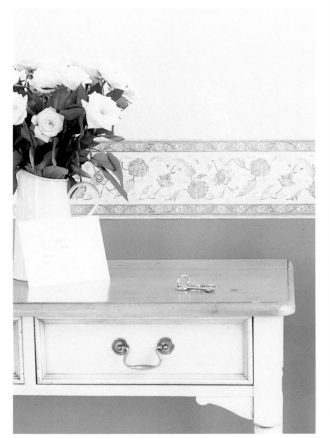

▲ You don't need to put up a dado rail – just use a decorative wallpaper border to divide your wall visually.

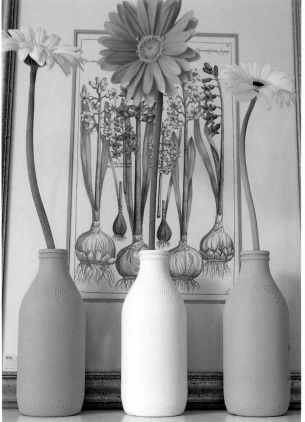

▲ Paint empty bottles in pastel shades and use them as vases along a windowsill or mantelpiece.

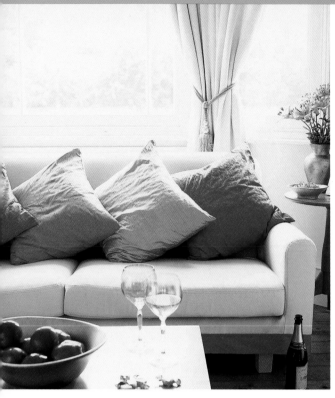

▲ Change the look of a neutral sofa with a row of fat silk cushions.

# Rich, warm tones

Burnt orange and sepia complement each other well and add warmth and richness to a neutral colour scheme. Orange, in all its various shades, makes a particularly good accent colour.

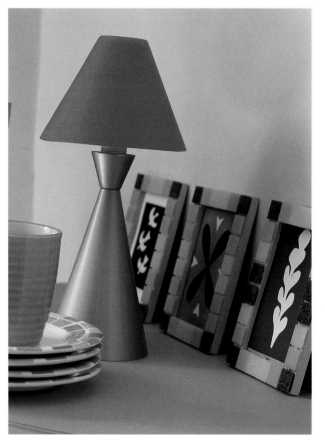

▲ Glue coloured glass mosaic tiles to plain wooden picture frames to make them part of your decorating scheme. Use tiles of contrasting colour at each corner.

▲ Update the traditional line-up of family photos by grouping black and white snaps together on a mantelpiece.

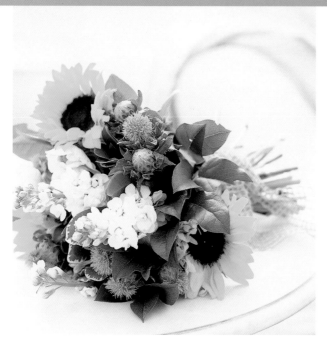

▲　Fresh flowers transform a room. Pick blooms in colours to suit your scheme.

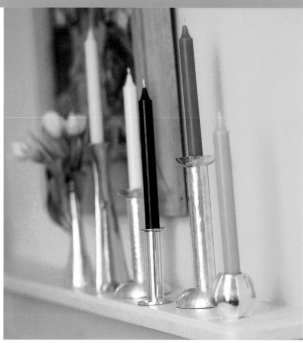

▲　Turn a simple row of candles into a focal point by swapping white ones for zesty shades.

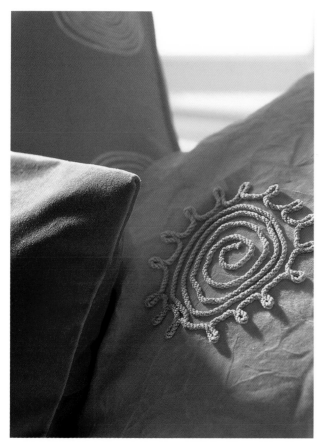

▲　Jazz up a plain cushion by curling a length of satin rope into a pattern and stitching it onto the cushion cover.

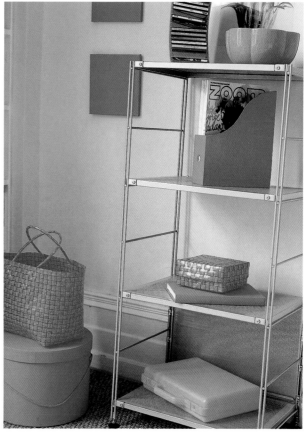

▲　Brighten up your room with coordinated storage magazine files, CD holders and knick-knack boxes.

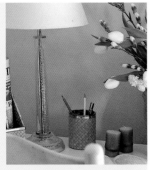

▲ A classic look doesn't need fussy details – just accessories in natural materials like wood plus a touch of silver metal.

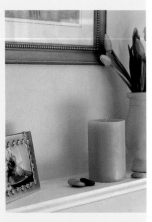

▲ The picture frames are inspired by the fireplace surround. Wooden frames echoing the floor would work, too.

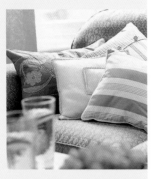

▲ Cushions in a mix of patterns make the sofa look inviting and give the room an informal air.

# Modern classic style

Create a timeless room with greens and yellows, blended with soft whites for a fresh feel.

Relaxing green and sunny yellow make a great partnership in this living room with its dramatic fireplace and tall, traditional windows. You could match the walls to the muted green of the sofa, but using a fresher shade makes the room more vibrant. It's the yellow curtains, however, that really bring the whole room to life with one bold injection of colour. All that's then required are just a couple of splashes of yellow on the cushions and flowers.

Matching furniture can look a bit formal, so for a more casual feel, try mixing your sofa with an armchair in a different fabric. Subtle pattern on the floor-length curtains, sofa and rug give the room the touch of detail that a classic scheme needs. Finally, choose off-white for the woodwork, furniture, fireplace and accessories to keep it all feeling fresh

## What else would work?

• pale, textured carpet
• tapestry cushions
• chenille or corduroy upholstery fabric

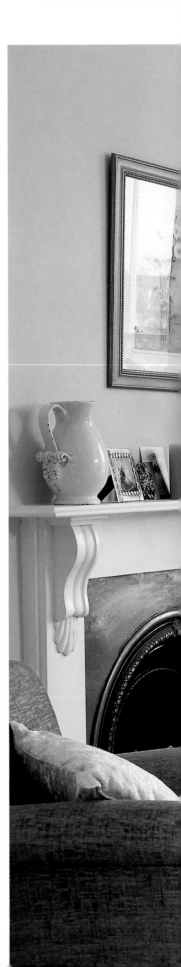

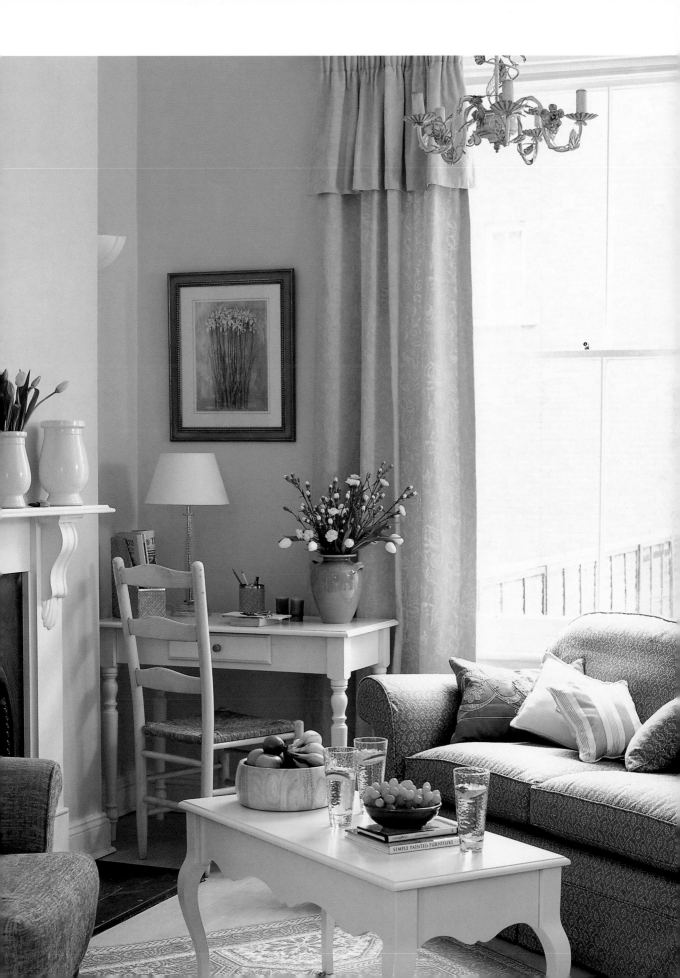

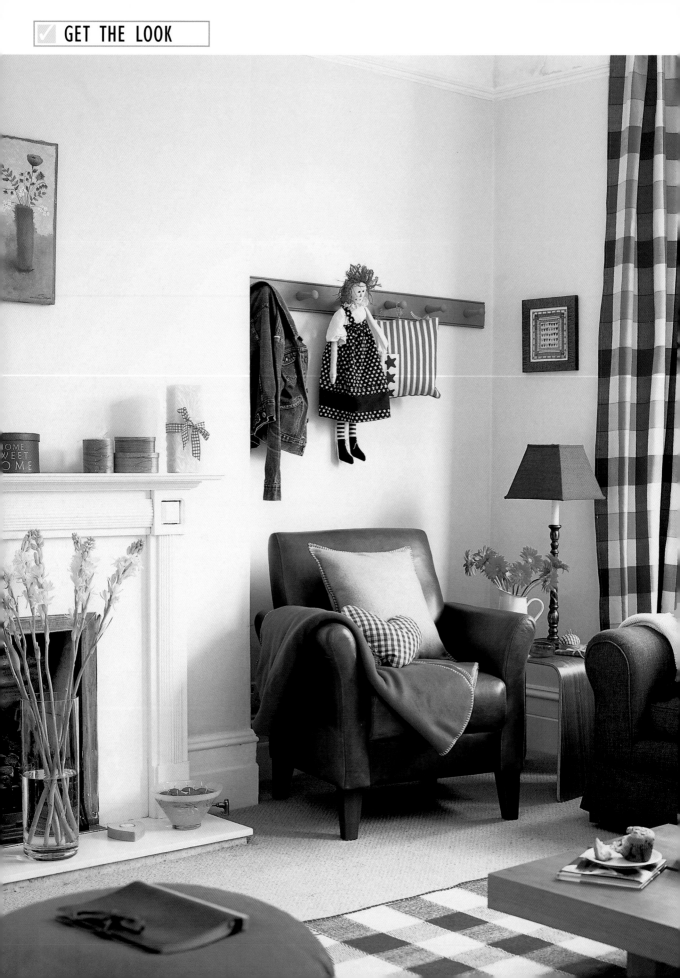

☑ GET THE LOOK

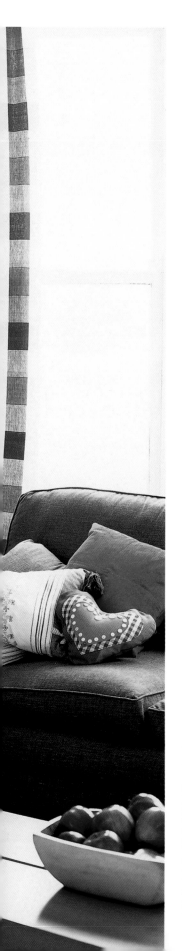

# Clean and crisp

## Use red, white and blue to create a smart but comfortable family living room.

This is a very simple but effective colour combination. Start with a completely neutral basic room with a natural carpet and off-white walls (pure white is too harsh and clinical, so try a white with the tiniest hint of mushroom) and let the furnishings add the colour. Use blue as the main colour and warm up the whole room with a scattering of red such as a lampshade, cushions, candles and footstool.

Primary colours like red and blue can look as though they belong in the nursery so choose a strong but slightly faded denim blue and a rich red for a more sophisticated result. Finally, give your room personality with a hint of an American country theme – bold checked curtains and a matching rug, a Shaker-style peg rail, folk art picture print and gingham heart-shaped cushions.

### What else would work?

- blond wood furniture
- seagrass carpet
- stripes instead of checks

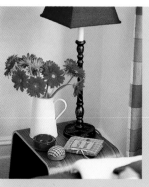

▲ Stick to red, white and blue or dark wood accessories to keep it feeling unfussy.

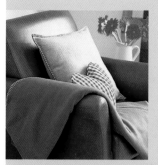

▲ Leather is a good choice for family rooms as it ages so well and looks good even with a few scuff marks. Add a soft felt cushion and throw to make it more comfortable.

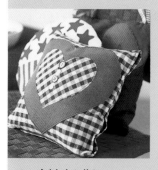

▲ Add detail to cushions with bold heart shapes stitched to the front and rows of buttons for extra texture.

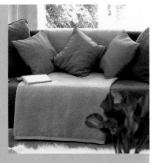

▲ Add extra cushions in a couple of paler tones to personalize your sofa.

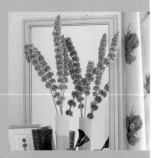

▲ One bold shot of contrasting colour is a great colour trick. Here, it's a vase of dramatic lime green stems.

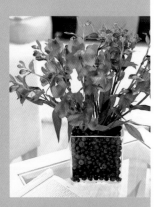

▲ Make flower arrangements part of your scheme. Arrange pink blooms in a glass tumbler, placed in a larger, square vase. The space between is filled with handfuls of blueberries.

# Dramatic berry tones

Blend edible shades of plum and raspberry for an easy-to-live with but sophisticated style.

This is a deceptively easy way to decorate a room because you are really decorating with only two basic colours – cream and plum. The trick is to use many shades of plum – from the deep sofa colour to soft lilac with raspberry pinks in between. Deep plum might seem a risky colour choice, but think of it more as an original alternative to navy, then use plenty of raspberry to brighten it up. Set it against cream walls to make the room feel light and airy. Contrast the contemporary sofa and armchairs with cream, country-style wooden furniture.

Make the windows a focal point with layered curtains. Use a bold print fabric as dress curtains at either end of the curtain rail – since they are not designed to draw across the window, you need less fabric than normal so you can use a more expensive fabric. Then pick out the main colour in the print for heavy, plain curtains that do the job of drawing across the window.

## What else would work?

• soft furnishings in blues from navy to forget-me-not
• silver accessories
• dusky pink carpet

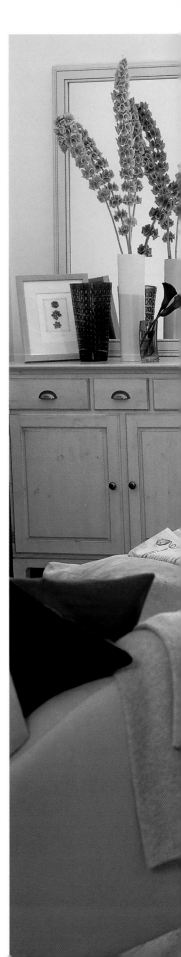

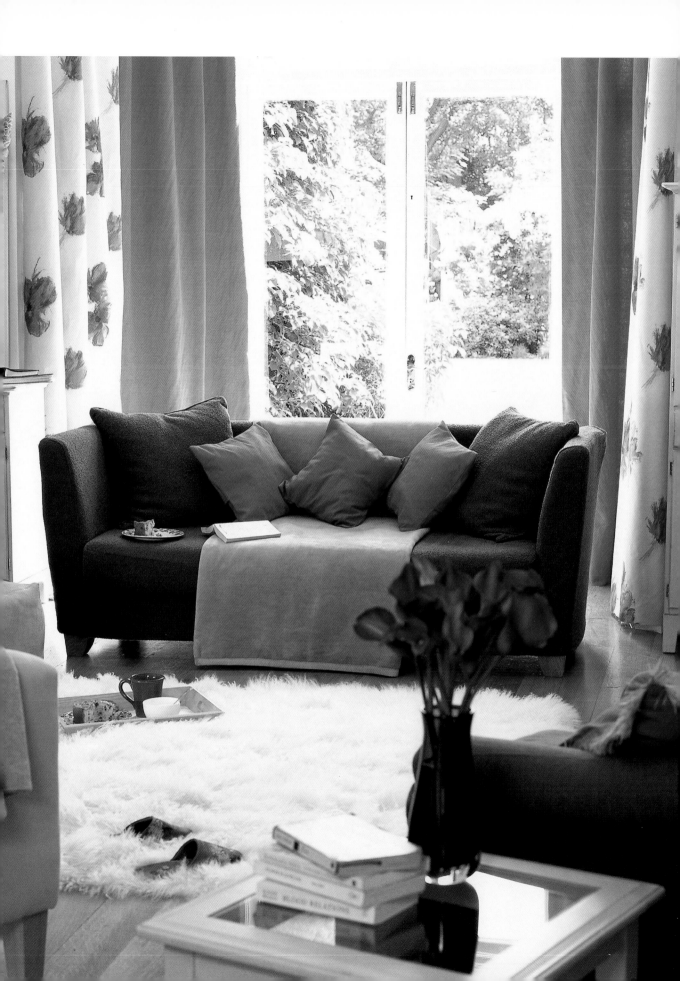

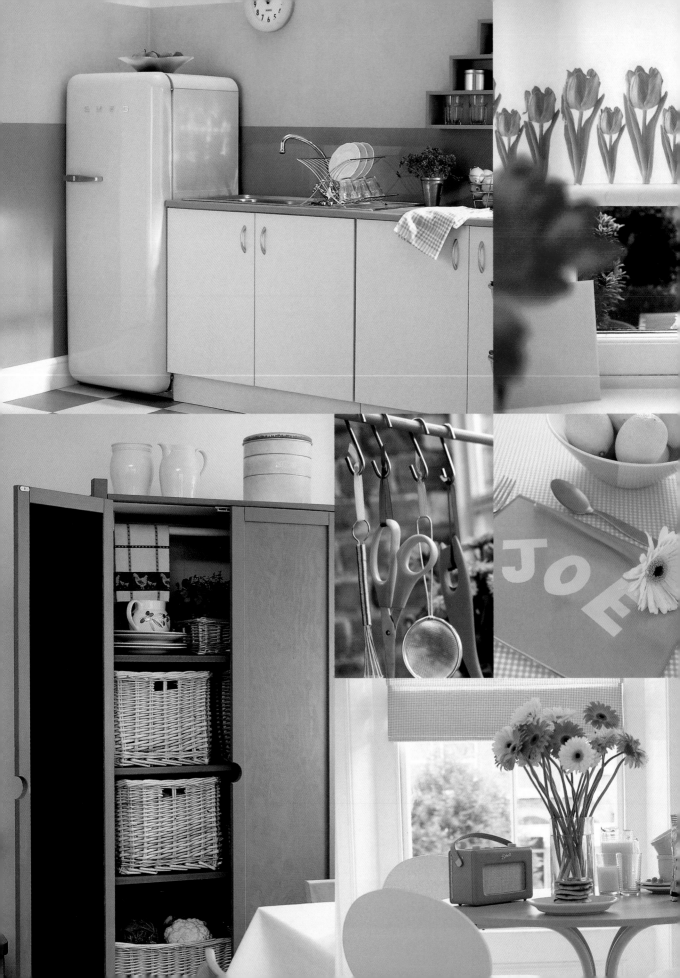

# Kitchen

The ideal kitchen has to be **well planned** and practical – easy to clean and pleasurable to **work in**, with everything you need to hand. Make **colour** the key to turning your kitchen from an efficient workplace into a room that is warm, creative and friendly. Since both floor and wall space tend to be smaller than in other rooms, you can be adventurous with colour. Be bold with colourful units, window treatments, worktops or simply with pots and pans.

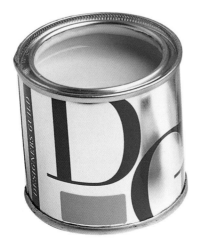

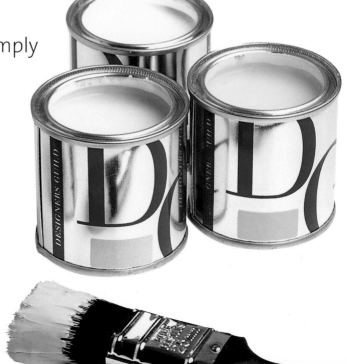

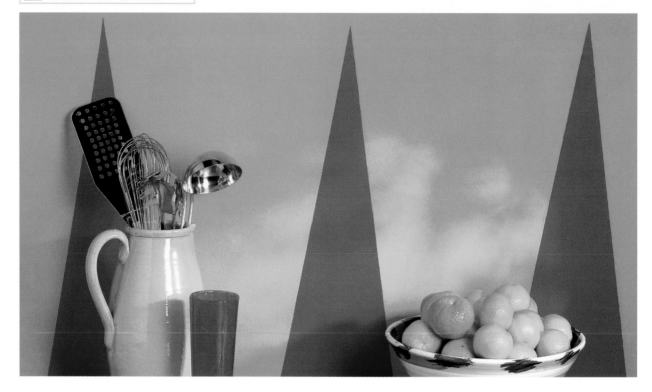

# Backgammon board style walls

Make the most of a small amount of wall space with this fun pattern of interlocking points. The finished effect is striking and gives the illusion of height in the space between wall units and the worktop.

**HOUR**
per wall
plus drying

**You will need**
- low-tack masking tape
- old newspaper
- emulsion paint in two colours
- household paintbrush
- pencil and spirit level

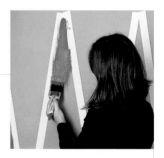

**1** Mask off the worksurfaces or lower part of the wall and protect with newspaper. Paint the wall in the lighter shade of emulsion paint. When the paint is dry, lightly draw a horizontal line, using the spirit level as a guide, to mark where you want the tips of the triangles to come. Plot where the triangles will be and mask off with the tape.

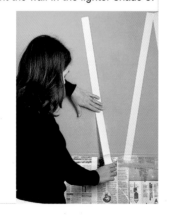

**2** Paint the deeper colour inside the masking tape. Leave to dry.

**3** Carefully peel off the masking tape when the paint has dried to reveal the full backgammon board effect.

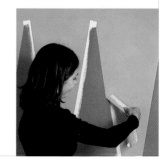

# Homemade wooden butcher's block

Transform a small pine table into a handy workstation by adding a shelf, hooks and rails. Attach screw-in castors to the table legs, if desired, to make it a mobile unit.

**3 HOURS**
plus drying

### You will need
- tape measure
- small bare pine table
- dust mask
- handsaw
- sheet of 18mm (¹¹/₁₆in) MDF
- pencil
- hammer and nails
- wood glue
- household paintbrush
- wood varnish
- 4 cup hooks
- 2 metal rails
- butcher's hooks

**1** Measure from the outside edge of one table leg to the outside edge of the leg to its right. Next measure from the outside edge of the same table leg to the outside edge of the leg to its left. You now have the measurements for the depth and width of the shelf. Wearing a dust mask, cut the MDF to these dimensions.

**2** Place the piece of MDF on the floor, stand the table on top, then draw around each leg with a pencil. Cut out each corner carefully.

**3** Hammer two nails into the inside edge of each leg on which to rest the shelf. Add a little wood glue to the legs for extra strength and sit the shelf on top.

**4** Varnish the entire table and shelf and leave to dry.

**5** Screw a cup hook into each corner of the table on two sides. On the opposite sides, fix the metal rails and attach butcher's hooks to finish.

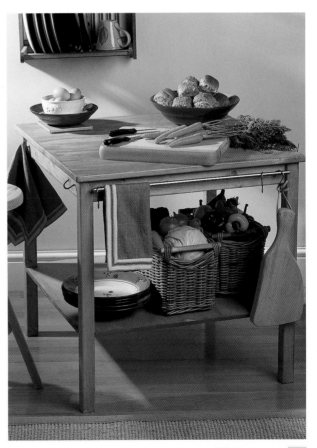

# Country-style larder unit

Turn a small wardrobe into essential kitchen storage by adding a few shelves and wicker baskets. Paint the inside of the doors with blackboard paint for a handy memo board.

**1** Using a spirit level and tape measure, draw lines inside the wardrobe where each shelf will go. If the wardrobe is very wide, or the baskets will be heavy, add battening to the inside back of the wardrobe as well as to the sides.

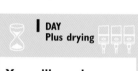

**DAY**
**Plus drying**

**You will need**
- old wardrobe
- spirit level
- tape measure and pencil
- handsaw
- wooden battening
- wood glue
- screwdriver and screws
- dust mask
- sheet of 12mm (½in) MDF
- MDF primer
- household paintbrushes
- vinyl matt emulsion paint
- blackboard paint

**2** For each shelf, cut two pieces of battening to equal the distance from the inside front to the inside back of the wardrobe. If battening is required across the unit back, cut to fit between the side battens. Dab wood glue at intervals along the length of the first piece of battening and stick the batten against the pencilled line. Hold for a few seconds, then screw the batten to the wardrobe carcass. Repeat for each batten.

**3** Using the inside depth and width measurements, work out the dimensions for each shelf. Wearing a dust mask, cut the MDF to size. Paint each shelf with MDF primer, then apply one or two coats of emulsion. When dry, put the shelves in, resting them on the battens.

**4** Paint the outside of the unit to match the shelves. Paint the inside of each door with blackboard paint to create memo boards. Leave to dry completely before adding suitable wicker baskets.

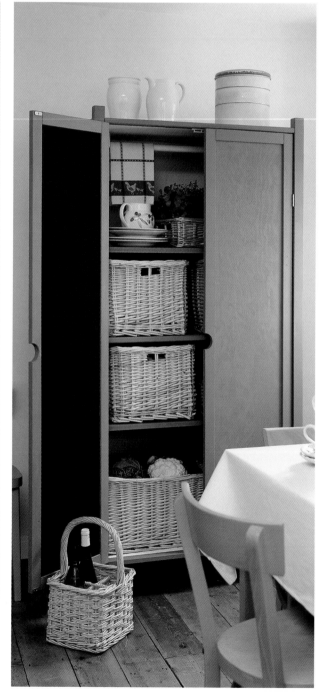

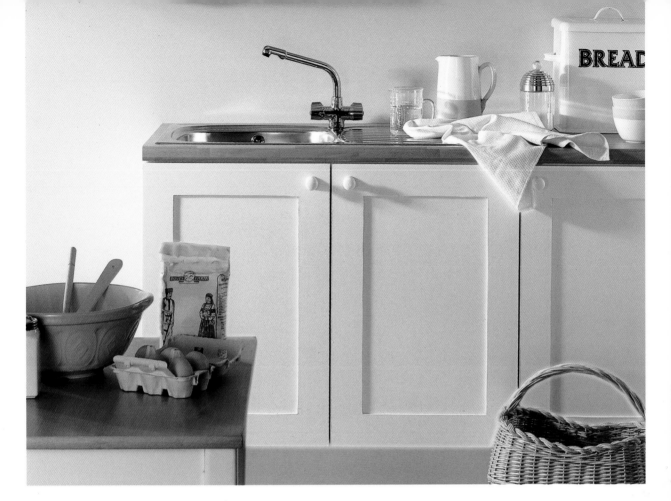

# Shaker kitchen units

Give plain doors a fashionable Shaker look with painted
frames of MDF and new wooden handles.

**2 HOURS**
per door
plus drying

### You will need

- screwdriver
- tape measure and pencil
- dust mask
- handsaw
- sheet of 6mm (¼in) MDF
- electric drill
- jigsaw
- sandpaper
- panel glue
- MDF primer
- household paintbrushes
- vinyl matt emulsion paint
- acrylic varnish
- wooden knobs

**1** Remove each door from its unit and measure its height and width. Wearing a dust mask, cut the MDF to the same size as the door. Mark out an 8.5cm (3¼in) border all round the MDF panel.

**2** Cut out the central panel of each MDF piece by first drilling a hole near each corner and then cutting out the piece with a jigsaw. Sand any rough edges, then attach the MDF border to the original door using panel glue. Leave under a heavy weight to dry.

**3** Paint primer all over the door. When dry, give each door two or three coats of emulsion paint, leaving the paint to dry thoroughly between coats. When completely dry, apply several coats of varnish.

**4** Sand the back of each knob, paint it to match the door, then varnish. Attach the knobs to the doors, then re-attach the doors to the units.

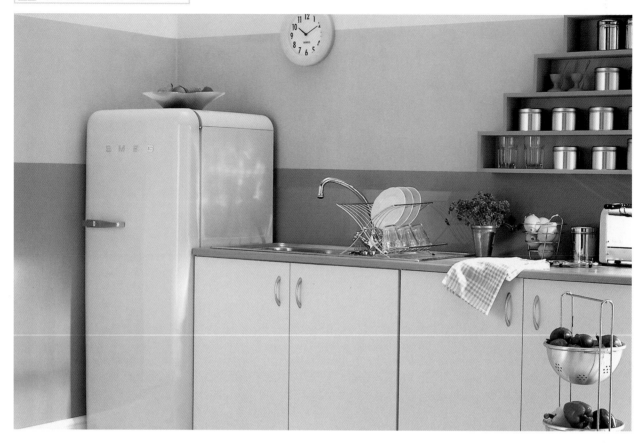

# Painted bands of colour

Using three or four shades of the same colour, paint wide bands of colour right round the room, graduating from dark to light, to give your walls extra interest and make the kitchen seem larger.

**2 HOURS**
per wall
plus drying

**You will need**
- vinyl matt emulsion paint in three or four colours
- household paintbrush
- pencil and spirit level
- tape measure
- low-tack masking tape

**1** Begin by painting the whole wall in the lightest colour. When the paint is dry, plan where you want the bands of colour to start and finish and pencil guidelines lightly on the wall using a spirit level to help. Start from one corner of the room and work outwards, then measure from the floor to the mark in each corner to check that the horizontal bands are level.

**2** Where two colours meet, mask off one band to prevent paint bleeding between the bands. Paint the deepest colour in the lowest band, then work upwards

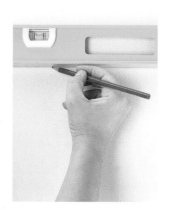

with the lighter shades, leaving each band of paint to dry before peeling off the tape and remasking to paint the next band.

# Revamped kitchen chairs

Turn a mismatched selection of ordinary kitchen chairs into a colourful set by painting them in bright colours. Careful preparation and finishing is the key to a good, lasting result.

**1** Prepare the chairs for painting as necessary. Bare wooden chairs should be treated where necessary with knotting solution and then primed. Painted wooden chairs should be sanded thoroughly and washed down with sugar soap. Varnished wood should be treated with chemical stripper and sanded.

**2 HOURS** per chair plus drying

### You will need
- old wooden chairs
- knotting solution and primer
- sandpaper
- sugar soap
- chemical paint stripper
- emulsion paint in three colours
- household paintbrushes
- quick-drying clear varnish

**2** When the chairs are prepared, smooth and clean, paint each one with one or two coats of emulsion paint. Leave to dry, then finish off with several coats of varnish to protect the paint.

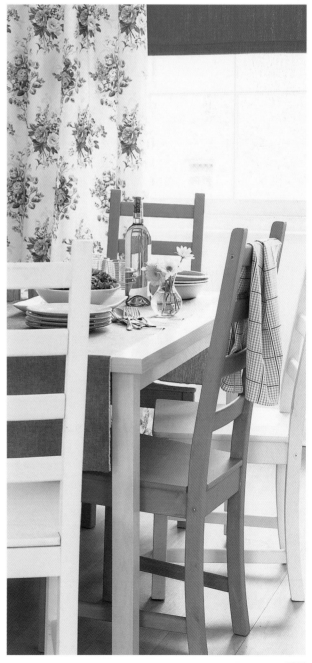

# Spring tulips

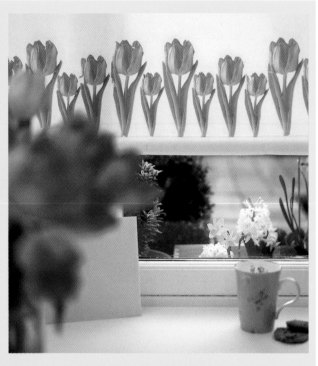

## Spots of colour

**2 HOURS**
per wall
plus drying

**You will need**
• pencil and spirit level
• emulsion paint in two colours
• household paintbrush

● Paint the wall, using the darker colour above the picture rail and the paler colour below. If you do not have a picture rail, draw a horizontal line, at picture rail height, mask off and paint as above to achieve the same effect. Use a pencil to mark out circles in a row, 5cm (2in) below the picture rail and evenly spaced. Use the darker paint colour and a small paintbrush to fill in the circles.

## Tulip transfer blind

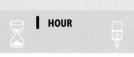

**I HOUR**

**You will need**
• image for colour photocopying
• fine scissors
• colour transfer gel
• plain blind
• wet sponge

● Choose an image that is easy to cut out, like the tulip used here, and colour photocopy it as many times as you need. Cut out the photocopied images and apply a thin layer of colour transfer gel to the front of each. Lay the images face down on the blind and leave to dry before rubbing the backing off with a wet sponge.

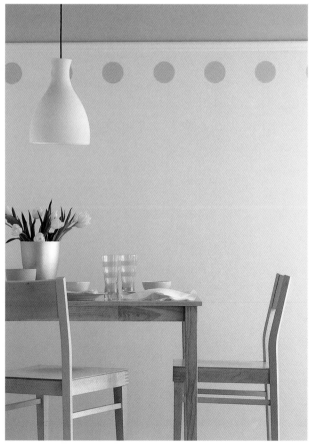

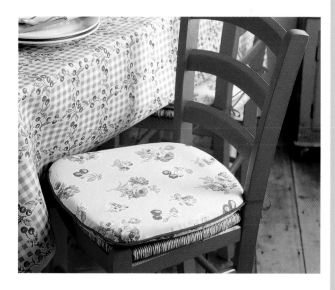

## Frosted glass jug

• Make your own stencil by first tracing your chosen image on to acetate. Cut out the image carefully using a craft knife to leave a stencil. Mount the stencil on to the jug using spray adhesive, then apply two coats of frosting spray. Allow to dry before peeling away the stencil.

**I HOUR**

**You will need**
• pencil
• sheet of acetate
• craft knife
• plain glass jug
• spray adhesive
• frosting spray

## Kitchen chair seat pads

• Measure the width and depth of the chair seat and draw a template on paper, adding 2cm (¾in) all round. Round the corners very slightly, then cut out the template. Lay the template on the seat and draw, then cut out, the two corners for the upright chair struts.

**I ½ HOURS**
**per pad**
**plus drying**

**You will need**
• tape measure
• pencil and paper
• scissors
• length of fabric
• dressmaker's pins
• sewing machine and/ or needle and thread
• piping (optional)
• 2cm (¾in) thick foam pad
• short lengths of ribbon
• iron

• Fold the fabric in half, right side out, and pin the template on to the fabric. Cut around the template to get two identical pieces of fabric. Remove the template and place the two pieces of fabric together, right sides facing. Pin then stitch around three sides of the cover, incorporating piping within the seams if using, and leaving open the side that is shaped to go around the chair struts. Press the seams.

• Using the paper template, pin it on to the piece of foam and cut the foam to size. Insert the foam pad, then handstitch the opening closed, inserting ribbon ties into each corner. Make sure the ties are long enough to fasten around the chair struts.

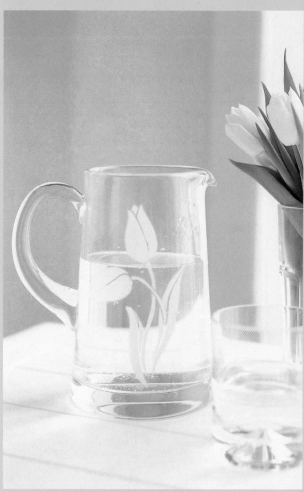

# Colourful stripes

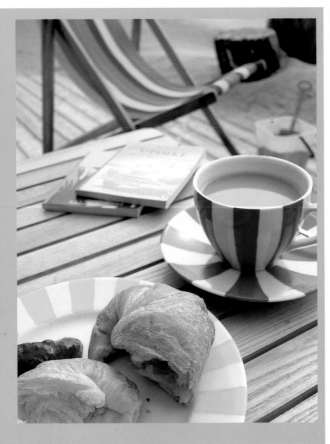

## Colourful utensil rail

• Cut dowelling to length and apply two or three coats of paint, leaving to dry between coats. Fix cup hook to wall to support dowelling. Cut short lengths of ribbon to loop through the handles of your utensils. Hang from butcher's hooks.

**2 HOURS** plus drying

**You will need**
• length of sturdy dowelling
• saw
• eggshell paint
• household paintbrushes
• 'S' hooks or butcher's hooks
• fine ribbon
• scissors

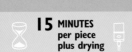

## Hand-painted china

• Paint deckchair-style stripes on plate edges, saucers and cups freehand using a small paintbrush and ceramic paint. Follow the manufacturer's instructions for using the paint – some ceramic paints need to be baked in the oven to set.

**15 MINUTES** per piece plus drying

**You will need**
• plain white china
• artist's paintbrush
• ceramic paint

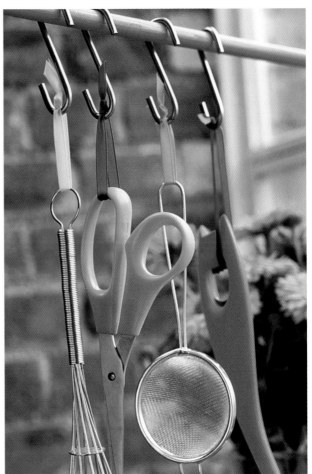

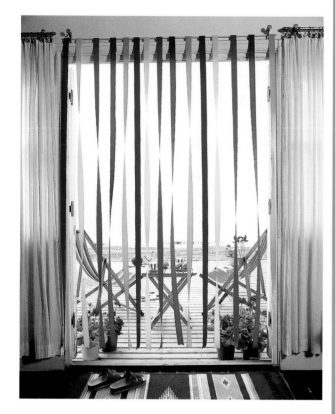

## Rainbow ribbon screen

• Hold a ribbon up to the top edge of the door frame to gauge the length required. Cut it to length, then use it as a template to cut the other ribbons to the same length. Cut a shallow

**20** MINUTES

**You will need**
• ribbon in five different colours
• scissors
• drawing pins

V-shape in one end of each ribbon to prevent fraying and pin the other end to the top edge of the door frame. (Alternatively, staple the ends of the ribbons to a light wooden pole using a staple gun and rest the pole on cup hooks above the doorway.)

## Tin can vases

• Soak the cans in warm, soapy water to get rid of labels and ensure they are very clean. Leave to dry. Paint all over with gloss paint. When the paint has dried, add stripes in contrasting colours.

**I0** MINUTES
**plus drying**

**You will need**
• old tin cans
• gloss paint in white, blue and yellow
• household and artist's paintbrushes

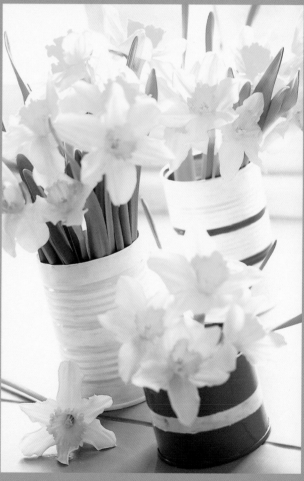

# Go square

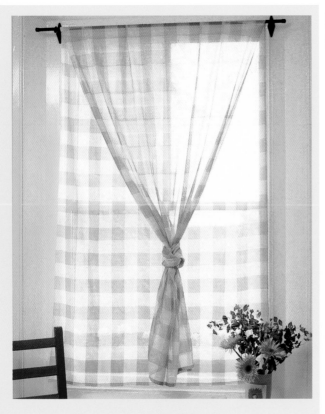

## Stencilled table runner

• Draw your desired pattern on to the stencil card and cut out the shapes using a craft knife. It is best to create two designs that can be alternated along the length of the table.

| ⏳ **1 ¹/₂ HOURS** plus drying |
|---|

**You will need**
- pencil and stencil card
- craft knife
- spray adhesive
- stencil brush
- woodwash

Apply spray adhesive to the back of the card and position it carefully on the table. Using a stencil brush, stipple the woodwash gently over the card. Don't load too much paint on to the brush – it is better to go over it two or three times to build up the depth of colour. Peel off the card and repeat on the next section of table.

## Voile window dressing

• Measure the height of the window from the curtain pole to the windowsill and cut the voile to twice this length, plus 10cm (4in). Hem the raw edges using iron-on hem webbing and press. Drape the fabric over the curtain pole, gather it up at the front and knot loosely as a decorative feature.

| ⏳ **30 MINUTES** |
|---|

**You will need**
- tape measure
- scissors
- length of voile
- iron-on hem webbing
- iron

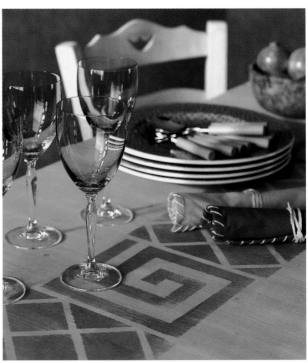

## Gallery wall

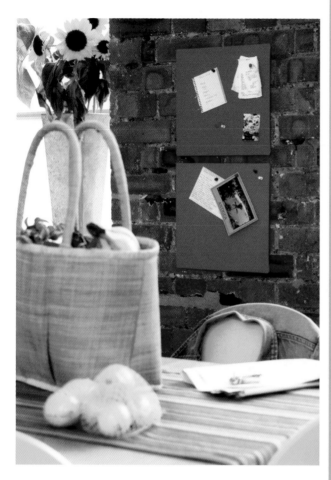

• Enlarge the picture images on a colour photocopier if necessary to fit the photo frames. Lay out the mirrors and photo frames on the floor to form a rectangular shape and adjust them until you are happy with the arrangement and spacing. Measure the overall size of the rectangle formed and mark its dimensions on the wall using a pencil and spirit level. Work out where the picture hooks or nails need to be for the edges of the pictures to fall along the marked lines.

**I HOUR**

**You will need**
• 7 brightly coloured images from a calendar or postcards
• 7 clip photo frames
• 7 mirrors
• tape measure
• pencil and spirit level
• hammer and nails or picture hooks

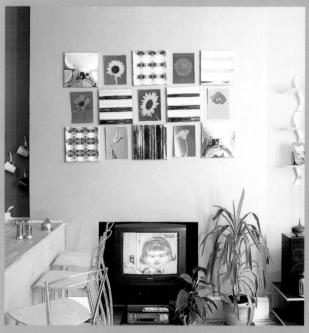

## Cork tile memo board

• Lay cork tile on to the felt and cut around, leaving a 2.5cm (1in) border. Spread glue all over one side of the cork tile, smooth felt on to the tile, turn over and glue overlapping felt on to the back of the tile. Fix to the wall with picture hooks or screws.

**20 MINUTES**

**You will need**
• cork tiles
• felt
• scissors
• strong all-purpose glue

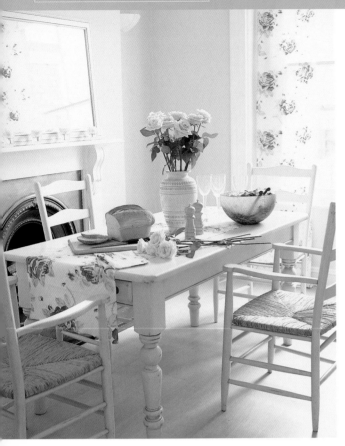

▲ Bring a floral theme to your kitchen by making coordinating curtains, tablecloth and napkins.

# Relaxed country style

Use assorted gingham and rose patterns in various guises – curtains, table linen, tea towels, storage containers – to achieve a country-style look for a roomy kitchen.

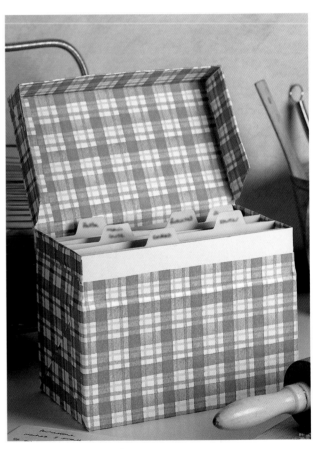

▲ Cover a flip-top box, such as an old washing powder container, with sticky-backed plastic and use it to file cards of your favourite recipes or addresses.

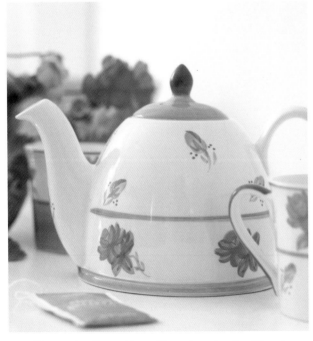

▲ Choose tea-time china with a charming traditional floral motif which won't date.

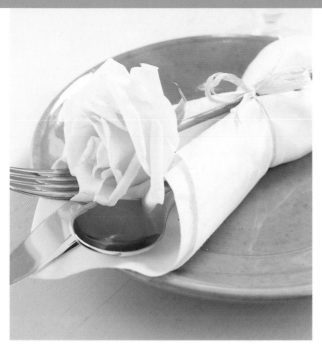

▲ Wrap cutlery in a white pressed napkin, tie them together with raffia and add a single bloom to make a memorable place setting.

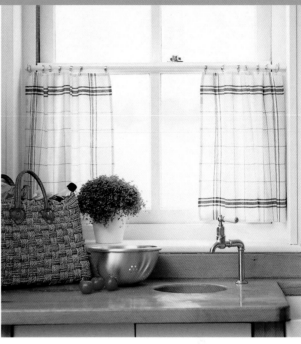

▲ Make café curtains from tea towels by attaching curtain clips to the tea cloths and slotting the clips on to a length of painted dowelling. Screw two hooks into the window frame to support the dowelling.

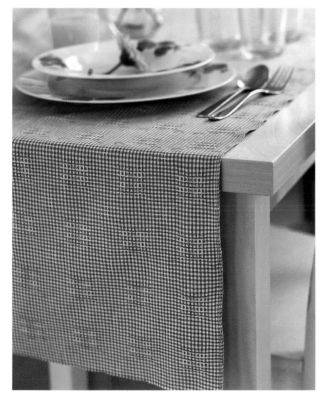

▲ Custom-make a table runner by hemming a length of fabric 60cm (24in) longer than the table and 10cm (4in) less than its width.

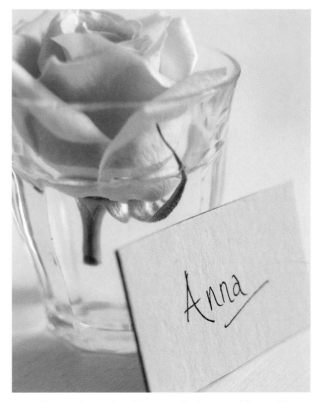

▲ Float a flower head in a small glass tumbler and lean a simple name card against it as a pretty place marker.

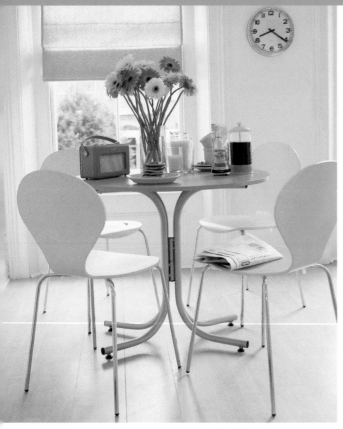

# Oranges and lemons

Bring a shot of bright colour to your kitchen with touches of orange and yellow. Cutlery, crockery, saucepans, chairs and curtains all offer possibilities for adding colour.

▲ Create a retro theme with bright yellow chairs, an orange 1950s-style radio and a vase of jaunty gerberas.

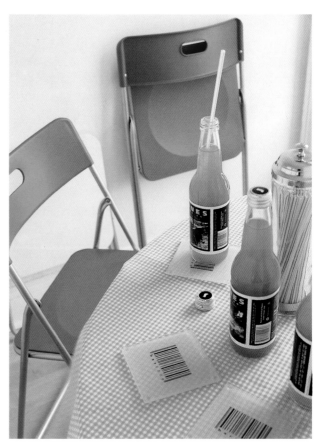

▲ Paste favourite recipes from magazines and newspapers into albums. Use a matching notebook to write down tips and recipes from friends and family.

▲ Fold-up chairs are ideal for kitchen dining as they take up next to no room when not in use.

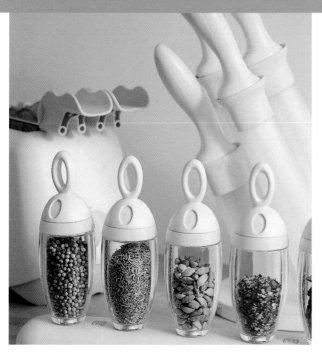

▲ Swap mismatched pots for a row of quirky jars containing colourful spices.

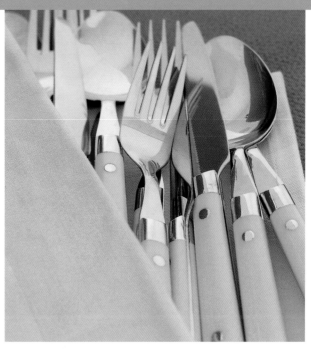

▲ Choose cutlery with brightly coloured handles to match your kitchen colour scheme.

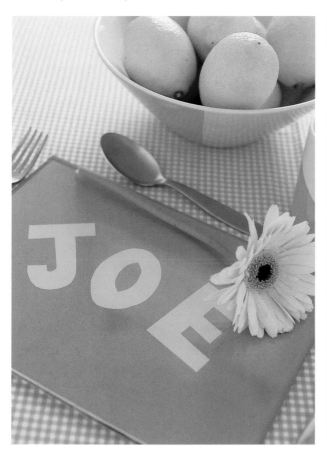

▲ Make individualized placemats for all the family. Cut names from a sheet of coloured paper, place over a second sheet and laminate.

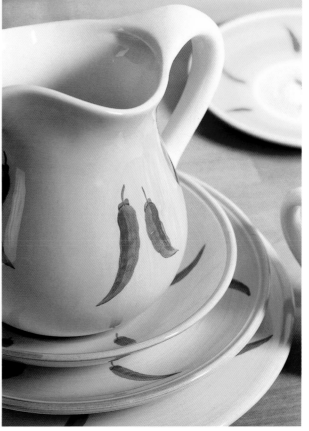

▲ A simple motif, like these chillies, running through the room adds an element of fun.

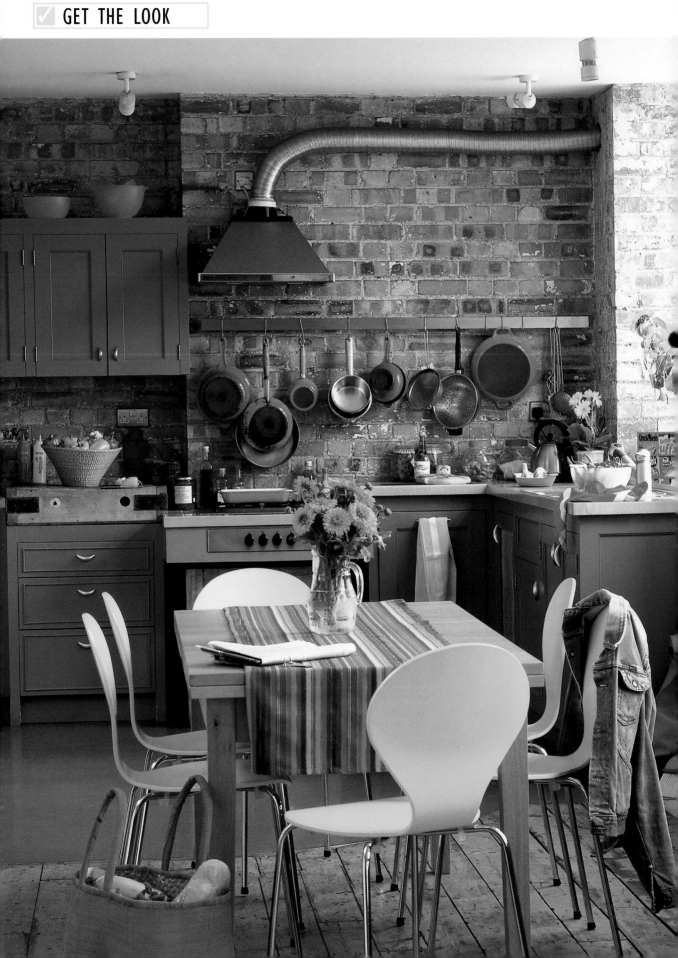

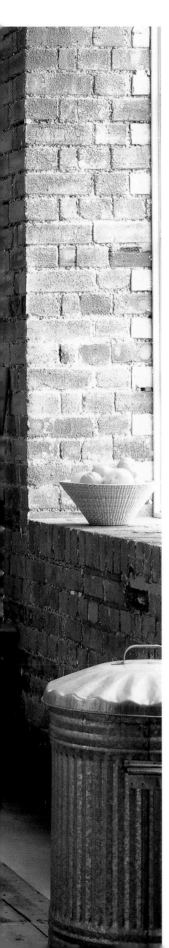

# Colours of Mexico

## Mix fiery reds and yellows reminiscent of South America with sea green paintwork.

Why worry about choosing a wall colour when stripping off the plaster to expose bare brick gives such a wonderfully textured terracotta backdrop? Use sea green paint on handmade MDF units to create the perfect partnership. You can then start to bring the room alive with bright, primary reds and yellows. Choose colourful pots and dishes and bright yellow chairs. Follow the red and yellow theme right down to details like the broom and the tea towels and the whole room will work better.

Keep everything else simple with stainless steel and chrome. Wooden worktops are a natural choice to go with the rough brick walls and the bare floorboards in the eating area, but although stripped pine floors look great, they are not practical for the cooking area. Instead go for vinyl, linoleum or the rubber flooring shown here. It's easy to clean and comes in a huge range of colours.

### What else would work?

- beech chairs
- whitewashed walls
- royal blue units
- beech venetian blind

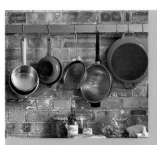

▲ A rail for pans frees up cupboard space and lets you make a show of colourful enamel pans.

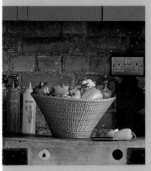

▲ Even fruit and vegetables can become part of your kitchen's look. Bowls of sweet peppers or lemons are great for adding colour.

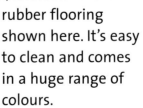

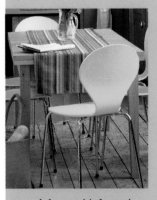

▲ A fun and informal multi-coloured tablecloth adds to the lively look of the kitchen.

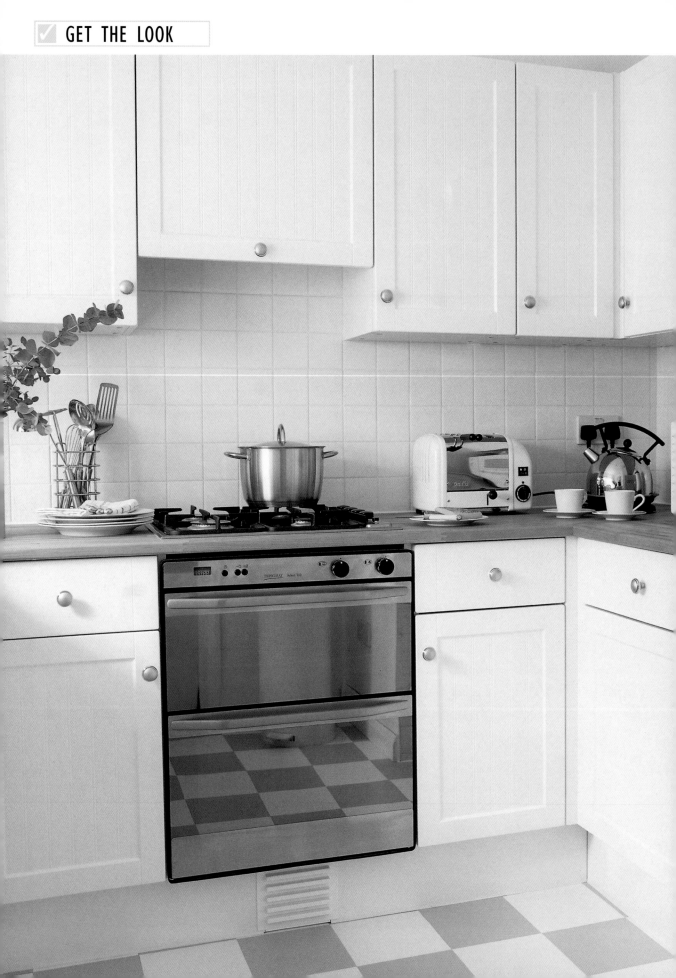

# Dazzlingly simple: white and steel

## Fill a tiny kitchen with light and a sense of space.

Reconsider what you regard as colour and you will recognize that in this kitchen wood, steel and white are as much a part of the colour scheme as the soft green floor tiles.

Use white units and splashback tiles to reflect as much light into the room as possible, making it seem bigger and brighter. Choose your whites carefully: there is an infinite variety of whites and this look depends on the units, tiles and grouting all being the same purest white. Keep all the appliances, utensils and pans in simple stainless steel so that they reflect even more light around the room.

Choose a different colour – such as beech – for your worktop. In a one-colour setting like this, it looks like a border running around the room. The chequerboard sage-and-white floor tiles bring an unexpected lighter touch to what could otherwise be a rather clinical-looking kitchen.

### What else would work?

- grey worktop
- white and blue enamelware
- soft blue chequered flooring
- ceiling spotlights

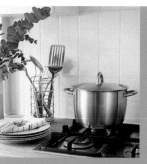

▲ Keep the scheme pure and simple with classic white tableware and chrome or white kitchen accessories.

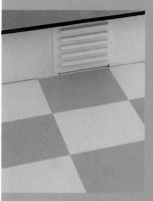

▲ The chequerboard design brings a livelier feel to the room, as well as adding an important touch of colour.

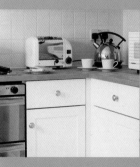

▲ Choose appliances that echo the white and steel theme.

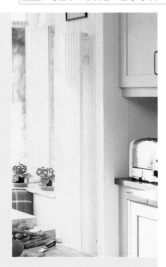

▲ Short of wall space? Heat your kitchen with an ingenious tall radiator which will fit on the slimmest of walls.

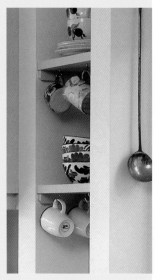

▲ An interesting alternative to wall units, alcove shelving can be built in simply and doubles as storage and display space.

# Summertime all the time

## Primrose yellow and warm wood combine to create a sunny, vibrant kitchen.

Feel uplifted every time you walk into your kitchen by painting timeless Shaker-style units in a soft yellow which makes the room feel spacious but warm. Add a modern twist and swap traditional wooden knobs for sleek brushed steel handles. Crisp white walls give the kitchen a clean, fresh feel while a soft grey laminate worktop is teamed with a grey slate floor – and both are smart but practical finishes.

Add cheery, colourful touches to make the room more welcoming: a yellow and white checked roller blind at the window, pretty pots of spring flowers along the windowsill and chunky hand-painted crockery.

In a kitchen with plenty of floor space, try using one small table paired with a mobile butcher's block which can be wheeled over to where you are working or pushed against the table to double the space you have for casual eating.

### What else would work?

- bamboo blind
- terracotta and wood accessories
- pale blue units

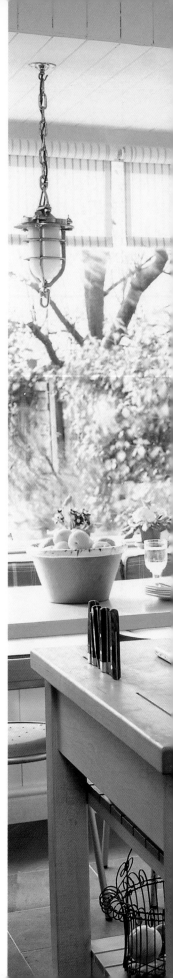

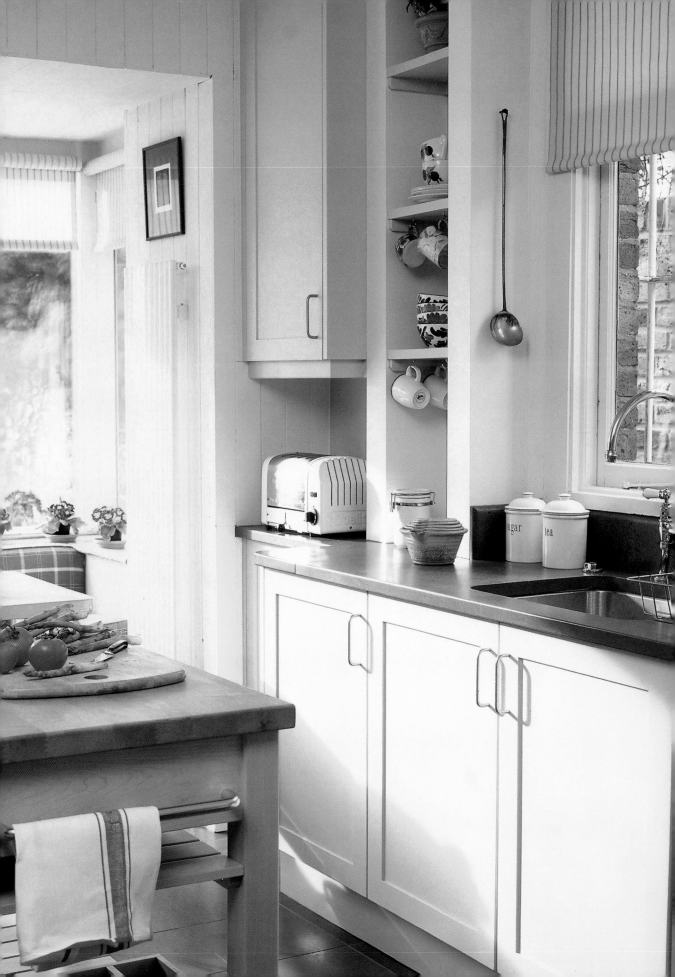

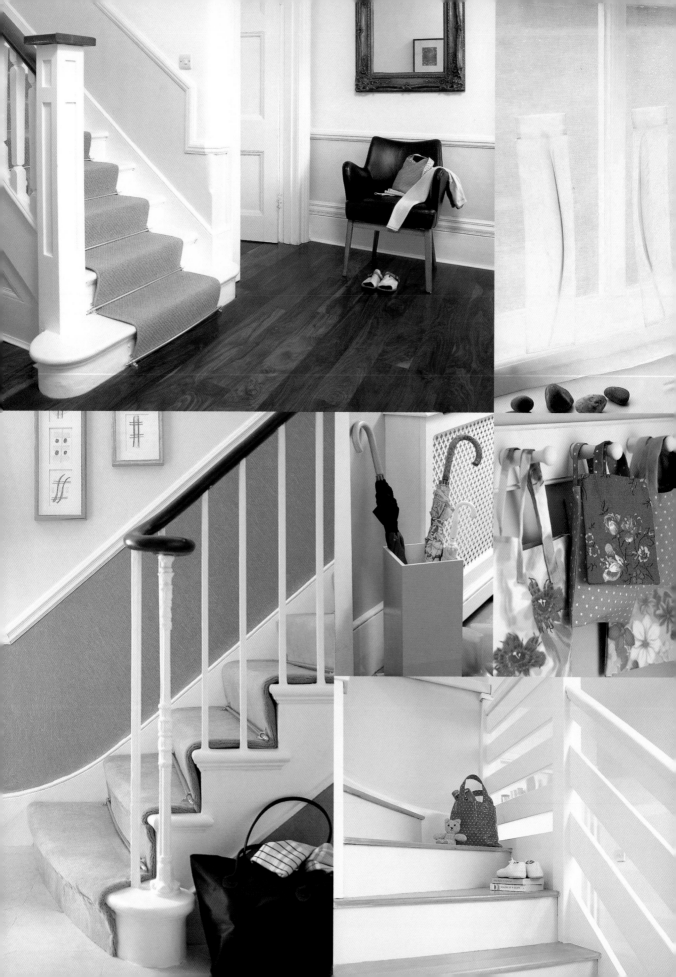

# Hallway

Hallways are so often neglected – left as uninspiring and gloomy corridors when they should be an **introduction** to your **home**, not just for visitors but for you, too. Every time you walk through the door, your hallway should make you feel happy to be home.

Because hallways tend to be short on natural light, warm, bright colours work well. Avoid anything too intense or dark but also white or very pale colours, which look dull in poor light. Floors need to be **hardwearing** and **mid-tones** work best, coping with dirt tramped in but not so dark that they make the floor space look smaller.

# Chunky panel walls

Give character and distinction to your hall with this new
version of traditional panelled walls. Save time and have
the wood cut to length at your builder's merchant.

**1** Measure the width of the
wall you want to panel. Cut
lengths of wood to cover
four times the wall width.
If there is a skirting board,
remove it.

⧗ **| DAY**

### You will need
- tape measure
- handsaw
- lengths of 1cm (³⁄₈in)
pine board
- 'liquid nails' glue
- pencil and spirit level
- set square
- matt woodstain
- household paintbrush

**2** Using 'liquid nails' glue,
fix the first length of wood
all the way along the wall,
tight to the floor as if fitting a skirting board. Fix the
second length over the first to create a double thickness
'skirting' all along the bottom of the wall. If the wall is
too long for single lengths of skirting, cut shorter
lengths and fix them so that the joins are staggered,
butting the pieces up to each other tightly.

**3** Fix the third length on the wall above the first, tightly
abutting them. Now mark how far up the wall you want
the finished panels to come. Mark this height using a
pencil and spirit level, all the way along the wall. Take a
plank and hold it against this line, flat to the wall and
draw underneath it all the way along the wall.

**4** Measure from the top of the third horizontal length to
the second pencil line. This is the length of the vertical
panel pieces. Work out what spacing will look best and
cut enough lengths to space out along the wall. Glue
them in place using the set square and spirit level to
check that they are perfectly vertical.

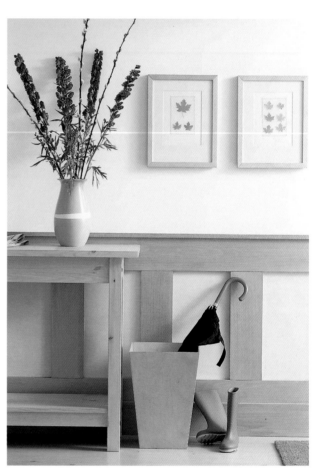

**5** Fit the final horizontal length all along the wall, resting
it on the vertical pieces. To finish, top the panelling with
one last length of wood, sawn in half lengthways and
fixed to the top piece of wood at right angles to create a
narrow ledge. Seal the panelling with matt woodstain.

# Trellis telephone table

Turn a simple wooden box or chest into valuable hallway storage space, giving you somewhere to sit and chat with a lift-up lid for telephone books and shoes.

**1** Unscrew the lid hinges and remove the lid from the chest. Saw the lid in half widthways to make two smaller lids. Sand the edges smooth and refix them to the box with two hinges each.

**2** Apply woodstain to the entire chest, inside and out, and leave to dry.

**3** Measure the inset panels of the chest and saw trellis panels to fit. Apply woodstain to the trellis, taking care to apply stain inside all the decorative shapes. Fix the trellis to the box using strong wood glue.

**4** Cut a piece of foam to fit one of the chest lids and fix it to the lid with foam glue. Cut a piece of fabric large enough to cover the foam and tuck underneath the lid. Stretch the fabric over the foam and staple it in place under the lid. Stitch or stick a decorative trim around the edge of the seat to finish.

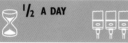

**½ A DAY**

## You will need
- screwdriver
- bare pine chest with lid and inset panels
- handsaw
- sandpaper
- 4 metal hinges and screws
- woodstain
- household paintbrush
- tape measure
- decorative trellis
- strong wood glue
- scissors
- piece of 6–8.5cm (2½–3¼in) foam
- foam glue
- length of fabric
- staple gun and staples
- needle and thread or craft glue
- decorative trim

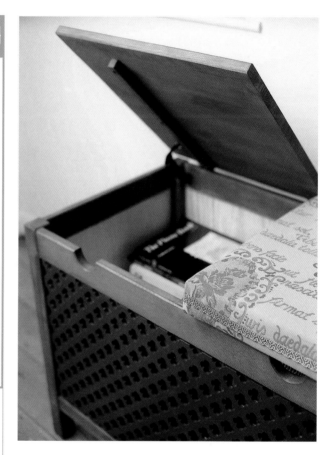

# Handy umbrella stand

**Make a sturdy and colourful umbrella stand that fits perfectly in your hallway.**

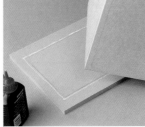
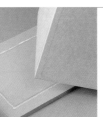

**1** Prime all five pieces of MDF all over and leave to dry. Using the paint chosen for the umbrella stand interior, paint each of the four side panels on one side only and along what will be the top edge of each piece. Paint one side of the base and all its edges in the colour for the exterior. Leave to dry.

**2** Take two of the side panels and, on the unpainted face of each, draw a line parallel with, and 6mm (¼in) from, each long edge. Tap panel pins in slightly at intervals along these lines, starting 4cm (1½in) from the bottom and ending 4cm (1½in) from the top.

**3** On the remaining two side panels, apply weatherproof wood glue all along one long edge.

**4** With the painted faces all facing inwards, position one pinned panel against the glued edge of one side panel and hammer into place. Repeat with the other glued side panel. Glue the remaining long edges and hammer the final panel into place. Leave the glue to dry before filling any gaps with wood filler and sanding smooth.

**5** Position the frame in the centre of the painted base and mark a pencil line around the inside edge. Apply glue along the outside of the line, then stand the frame

in place. Top with a heavy weight, such as books, and leave to dry. To finish, paint the outside of the holder all over with the exterior colour and leave to dry upside down.

⏳ **3 HOURS** plus drying

### You will need
- MDF primer
- household paintbrushes
- sheet of 12mm (½in) MDF, cut as follows:
4 rectangles, 20 x 45cm (8 x 18in), for the sides;
1 square, 25 x 25cm (10 x 10in), for the base
- oil-based paint in two colours
- ruler and pencil
- hammer and 2.5cm (1in) panel pins
- weatherproof wood glue
- wood filler
- sandpaper

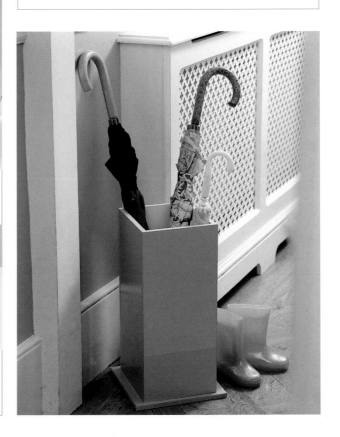

# Shaker shelf with mirror

This useful mirror is also a handy shelf for posies, post or spare change. Omit the shelf and add hooks for keys or adjust the size of the frame to suit your hall.

**3 HOURS** plus drying

**You will need**
- pencil and tape measure
- 40 x 60cm (16 x 24in) rectangle of 18mm (1¹⁄₁₆in) MDF
- dust mask
- jigsaw
- wood glue
- screwdriver
- 2 x 20mm (³⁄₄in) screws
- sandpaper
- MDF primer
- household paintbrushes
- oil-based paint
- strong adhesive
- 30 x 50cm (12 x 20in) mirror
- 2 screw eyes and picture wire

**1** Mark a 25 x 45cm (10 x 18in) rectangle in the centre of the piece of MDF. Wearing a dust mask, cut it out with a jigsaw. From the cut-out piece of MDF, cut a shelf 11.5 x 40cm (4½ x 16in). Cut away a

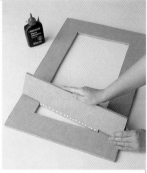

piece measuring 18mm (1¹⁄₁₆in) deep and 7.5cm (3in) long from either end of one long edge to leave a lip that will fit inside the frame. Position the shelf along the bottom edge of the frame, glue, then screw in place from the back, using one screw each side of the frame.

**2** Sand the edges of the frame and shelf. Prime all over with MDF primer and leave to dry before painting with oil-based paint. When dry, apply a second coat of paint.

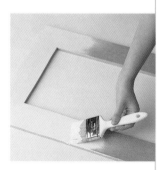

**3** Place the frame face down on a worktop with the shelf hanging over the edge. Apply strong adhesive to the back, no more than 5cm (2in) from the inside edge all round. Press the mirror face down on to the back of the

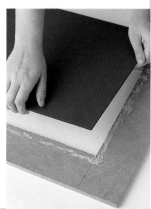

frame, weight down and leave to dry. Fit screw eyes to the back of the frame 10cm (4in) from the top edge and tie on picture wire to finish.

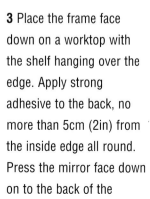

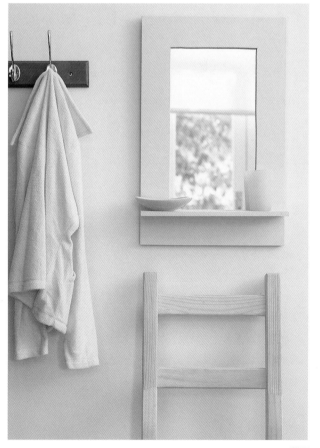

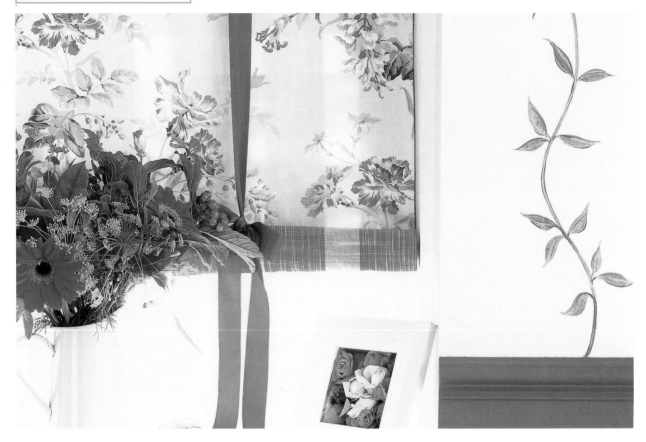

# Hand-painted leafy walls

Paint a dado rail and the wall beneath it in stunning red, paint the walls above in cream, then paint on a flowing, hand-drawn leaf design and suddenly your hall walls come to life.

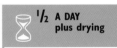 **¹/₂ A DAY plus drying**

**You will need**
- emulsion paint in red and cream
- household paintbrushes
- pencil
- scumble glaze
- artist's paintbrush

**1** Paint the dado rail and wall area beneath it in red, then paint the wall above in cream. When both are dry, use a pencil to draw a wavy line from ceiling to dado rail.

**2** Draw leaf shapes either side of the line and repeat the design at intervals along the wall. Mix one part red emulsion paint with three parts scumble glaze to

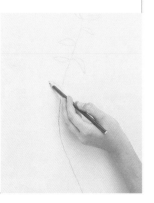

obtain a creamy textured paint that won't run. Using an artist's paintbrush, paint over the pencilled lines and fill in the leaf shapes, varying the strokes to get a textured effect on each leaf.

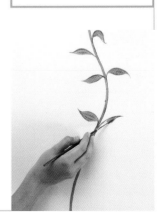

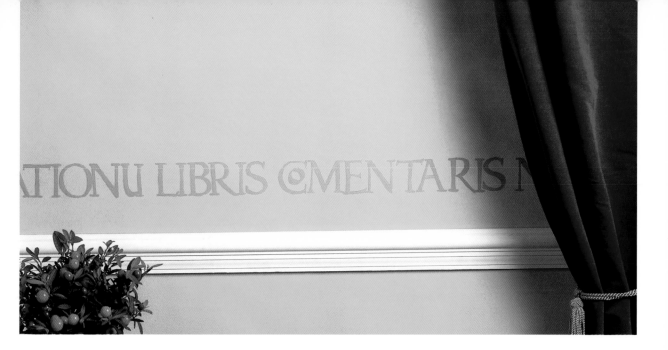

# Calligraphy frieze

Enliven an entrance with lettering that runs along the length of the hall. Use Latin for its shape and form or choose a favourite line of poetry to give visitors something to talk about.

**½ A DAY**

**You will need**
- soft pencil
- book of lettering
- tracing paper
- spirit level
- low-tack masking tape
- acrylic metallic-look paint
- fine artist's paintbrush
- clean soft eraser

**1** Trace the letters from a lettering book on to tracing paper. You can either trace out every letter of the alphabet and use as needed or trace all the wording you wish to use.

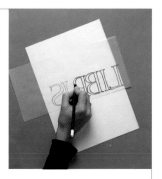

**2** Turn the tracing paper over and go over the letters again on the wrong side with the soft pencil.

**3** Draw guidelines on to the wall using a spirit level to ensure that the lettering will be level. Attach the tracing paper to the wall, right side out, using low-tack masking tape. Gently rub over the line

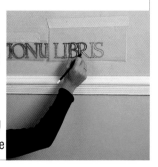

of each letter with the pencil to transfer the outline on the wrong side on to the wall.

**4** Remove the tracing paper and start to paint over each letter, using a fine artist's paintbrush and acrylic metallic paint, moving from left to right if you are right-handed and from right to left if you are left-handed. Once the paint has dried, use a soft eraser to remove any remaining pencil marks.

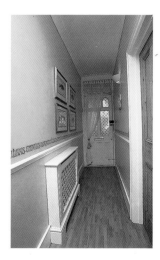

# Yellows and greens

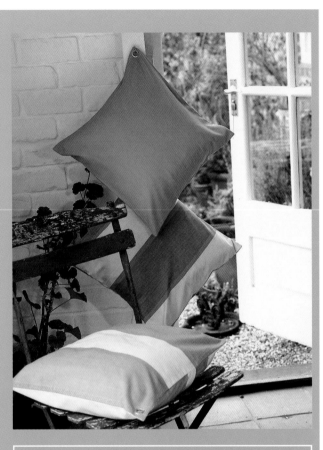

## Frosted dragonfly mirror

• Position the stencil on the corner of the mirror and attach with masking tape. Apply frosting spray and allow to dry before peeling away the stencil.

⧗ **10** MINUTES

**You will need**
• stencil of dragonfly or other image
• plain mirror
• masking tape
• frosting spray

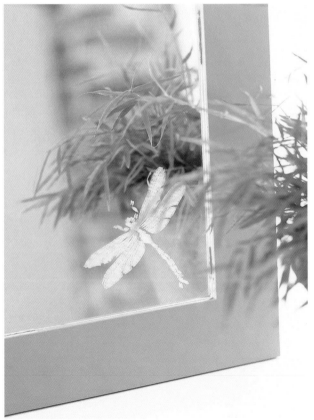

## Store garden cushions

• Punch a metal eyelet through one corner of each cushion. Drill holes into the wall or door frame and screw in cup hooks. Hang the cushions from the hooks – they are now stored handily by the door for when you want to take them outside.

⧗ **10** MINUTES

**You will need**
• eyelets and eyelet punch
• cushions
• electric drill
• cup hooks

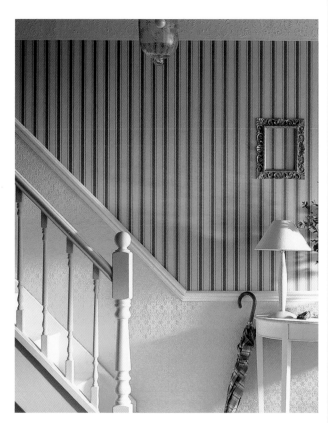

## Gilt-framed focal point

● Remove the backing and glass from the frames. Tap the nail into the wall to check where you want the frame to hang, then when you are satisfied with the positioning, hammer in the nail and hang the frame. Group matching frames in pairs, rows of three or squares of four.

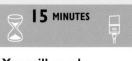

**15 MINUTES**

**You will need**
- old picture frames
- hammer and nails

## Two-tone wallpapering

● An imperfect wall is easily disguised with textured and patterned wallpapers. Cut the two wallpapers to size for above and below the dado rail and paste it to the wall.
Paint the textured wallpaper below the rail with an oil-based paint for a hardwearing finish. Match the paint to one of the colours in the stripe above for a smart look.

**¹/₂ A DAY**

**You will need**
- wallpaper scissors
- striped wallpaper
- textured wallpaper
- wallpaper paste and brush
- oil-based paint
- household paintbrush

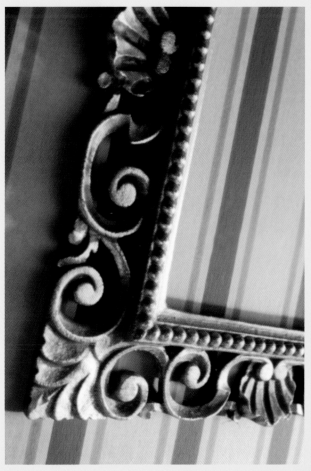

# Neutrals and naturals

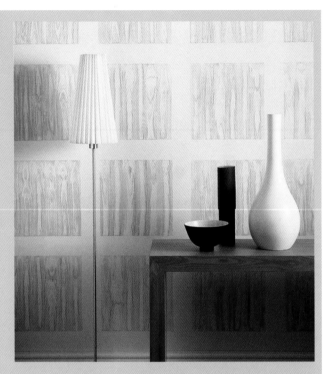

## Leaf border blind

● Trace a leaf motif on to tracing paper, then transfer the design to run along the bottom edge of the blind. Punch out holes at intervals along the pencilled lines with a carpenter's awl. Rub out any remaining pencil lines as you go.

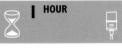

**I HOUR**

**You will need**
- pencil and tracing paper
- plain roller blind
- carpenter's awl
- clean soft eraser

## Textured checked wall

● Using the spirit level and masking tape, mark out squares over the entire light-coloured plain wall. Pour emulsion paint into the paint tray and dilute by half with water. Load the roller with paint, roll off the excess on kitchen paper, then roller over the squares. Leave the paint to dry before peeling away the masking tape.

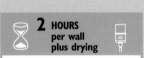

**2 HOURS per wall plus drying**

**You will need**
- spirit level
- wide low-tack masking tape
- emulsion paint
- paint tray
- water
- textured roller
- kitchen paper

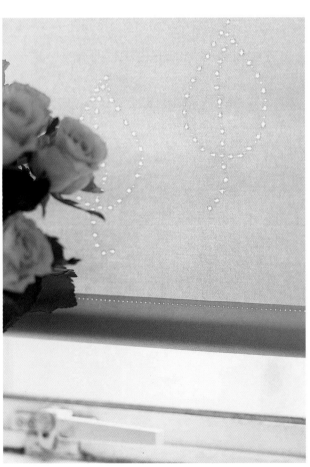

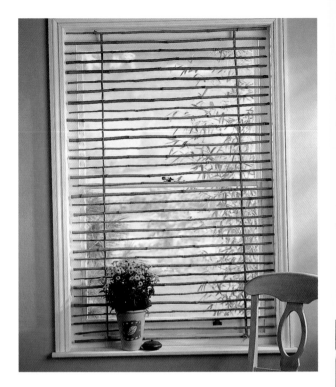

## Coat hook panels

• Wearing a dust mask, cut the MDF into a number of 40 x 120cm (16 x 47in) panels. Space out the panels along the wall, drill holes to take wallplugs and screw them in place. Paint the panels with woodstain or cover them with textured wallpaper. When dry, fix coat hooks on each panel.

**2 HOURS**

### You will need
- dust mask
- handsaw
- sheet of 12mm (½in) MDF
- tape measure and pencil
- electric drill and wallplugs
- screwdriver and screws
- woodstain or textured wallpaper
- coat hooks

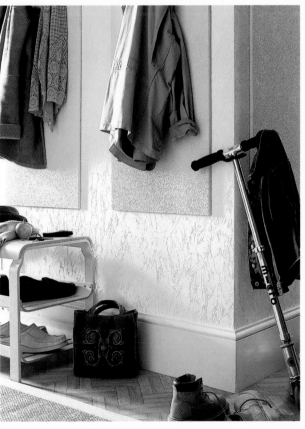

## Bamboo and copper blind

• Cut the bamboo canes to the width of your window and work out how many widths you need to cover the window, when placed at 2cm (¾in) intervals.
Cut the plastic tubing into 2cm (¾in) lengths. You will need double the number of pieces of plastic tubing as

**2 HOURS**

### You will need
- hacksaw
- bamboo canes
- tape measure
- narrow plastic tubing
- metallic copper spray paint
- scissors and string
- cup hooks

cane widths, minus two. Spray the tubing pieces with copper paint.

• Cut two lengths of string, each two-and-a-half times the height of the window. Fold both pieces of string in half, loop each one over what will be the top cane and knot to secure it, a quarter of the way in from each end of the cane. Thread the doubled string through a piece of tubing. Take a second cane, place it below the first, knot in place and thread on a tube in the same way. Repeat for all the canes. Hang the finished blind over two cup hooks screwed into the wall above the window.

# Stylish touches

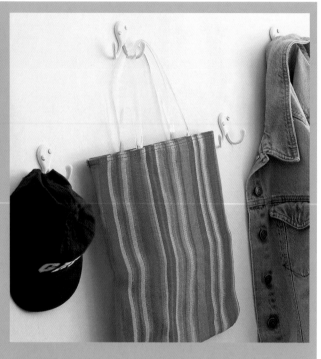

## Useful radiator shelf

- Position the shelf above the radiator and mark where the brackets need to go. Drill holes, insert wallplugs and screw the brackets in place. Prime the wood before painting the shelf and the radiator to match the colour of the wall.

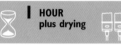 **I HOUR** plus drying

**You will need**
- narrow wooden shelf and brackets
- pencil
- electric drill and wallplugs
- screwdriver and screws
- primer
- household paintbrushes
- oil-based paint
- radiator paint

## Colour-matched hooks

- Plan where you want your hooks on the wall by putting blobs of sticky tack on the back of the hooks and moving them about until you have a design that works for coats, bags and hats at heights that are right for the whole family. Mark the position of each hook with a pencil.

 **20 MINUTES** plus drying

**You will need**
- metal double coat hooks
- sticky tack and pencil
- electric drill and wallplugs
- screwdriver and screws
- old newspaper and low-tack masking tape
- metal spray paint

- Drill holes where required, insert wallplugs, then screw the hooks in place. Mask the areas of wall around the hooks thoroughly, then spray paint the hooks the same colour as the wall.

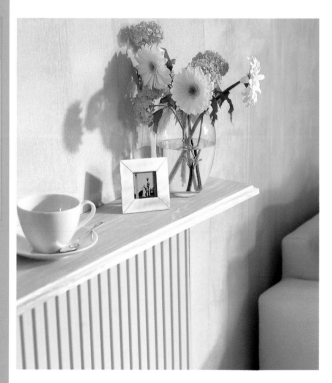

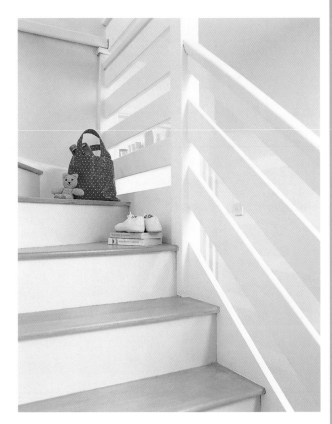

## Stylish draught excluder

• Roll up an old towel or blanket into a tight 'sausage'. Tie loosely with string to hold in place, then lay the 'sausage' in the centre of your remnant of fabric. Fold in the ends of the fabric and roll up to create a neat parcel. Secure tightly at each end with elastic bands and finish off with coordinating ribbon tied in a bow at each end.

**15 MINUTES**

**You will need**
• old towel or blanket
• scissors and string
• remnant of fabric
• heavy-duty elastic bands
• length of ribbon

## Painted stair risers

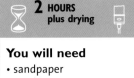

• Make sure each riser is clean and dry by sanding and washing down. Mask off the top and bottom edge of each tread to get clean lines when you paint and prevent bleeding. Paint the risers with one coat of paint and leave to dry. Apply a second coat if necessary. Remove the masking tape when the paint is dry.

**2 HOURS** plus drying

**You will need**
• sandpaper
• masking tape
• oil-based paint
• household paintbrush

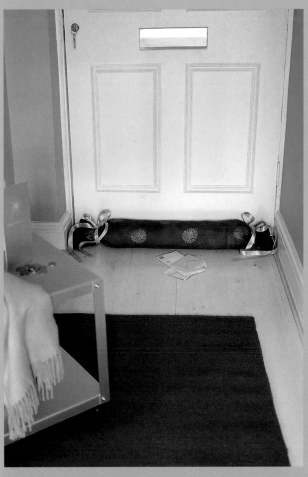

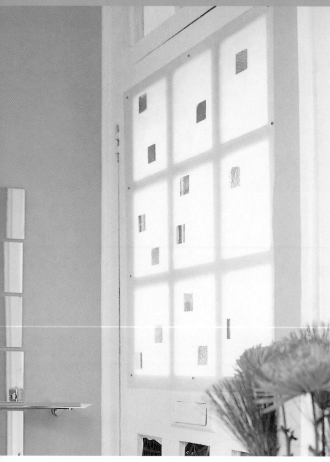

# A light touch

Go light and airy with fresh shades of green and white, while mirrors and glass enhance the feeling of light and space required for a welcoming hallway.

▲ Cut squares of masking tape and dot them over the front door windows. Frost the glass using frosting spray, then carefully remove the masking tape when dry.

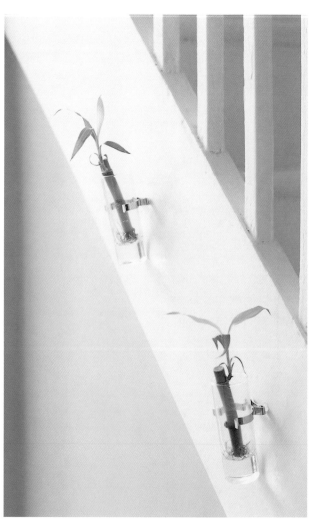

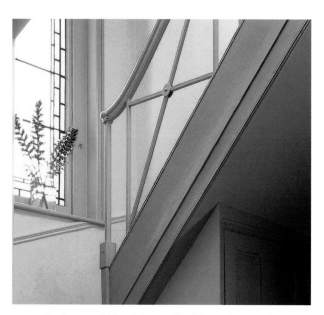

▲ Replace solid banisters with delicate ironwork to give the hall a more spacious, lighter feel.

▲ Even the tiniest hall can fit in these little test-tube vases. Line them up along the stairs with little pieces of living bamboo for best effect.

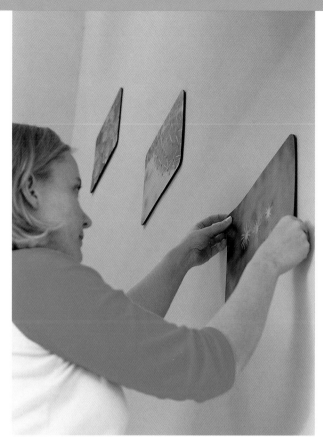

▲ Attractive placemats can become instant pictures up the stairs. Fix each one with four pieces of double-sided sticky tape.

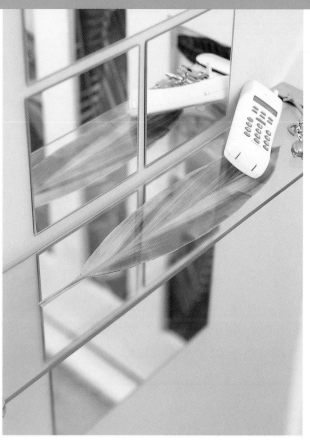

▲ Use mirror tiles fixed to the wall as an unusual hall mirror. Leave spaces between the tiles for the best effect. Add a glass bathroom shelf to finish.

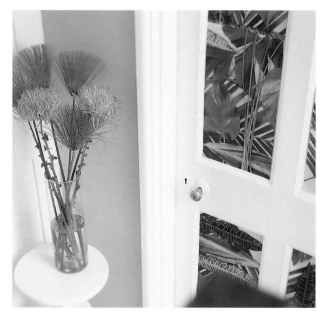

▲ Give old panelled doors a bit of personality by filling panels with bright, coordinating wallpaper or giftwrap strips, glued down and varnished to protect them.

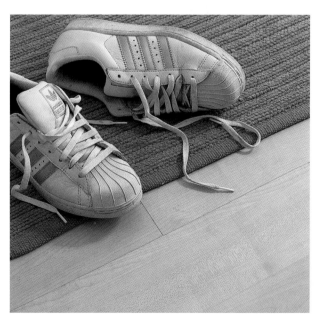

▲ You need an easy-clean floor in a hall. Laminate flooring is ideal, but warm it up with a bright runner.

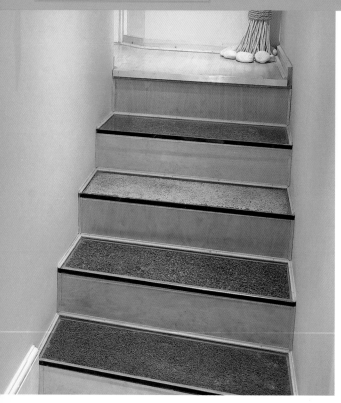

# Hall floors and walls

With a little do-it-yourself knowledge, some clever tricks and imaginative touches, you can bring your hallway to life.

▲ Turn stairs into a work of art by replacing the treads with reinforced glass and filling the steps with coloured gravel intended for fish tanks.

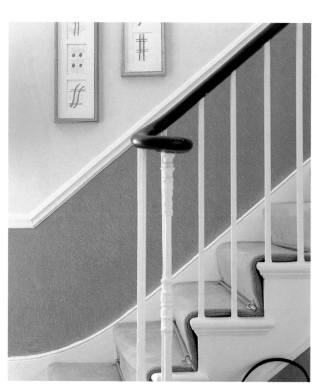

▲ Peg rails are perfect for hallways. Hang pretty bags as instant hideaways for clutter.

▲ Add a sense of timeless style with a runner up the stairs as an alternative to a fully fitted carpet. It is also far less noisy than bare wooden stairs.

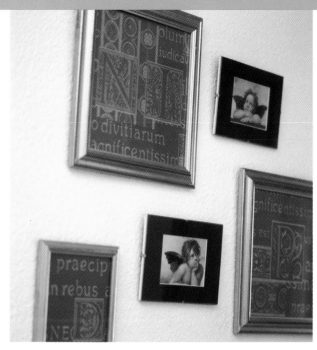

▲ Spray cheap pine frames with metallic gold paint and use to display your favourite fabric.

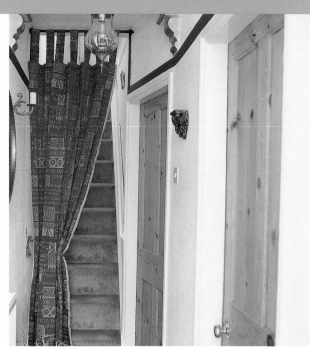

▲ In a hall where the stairs are directly opposite the door, break up the corridor effect by hanging a curtain at the foot of the stairs.

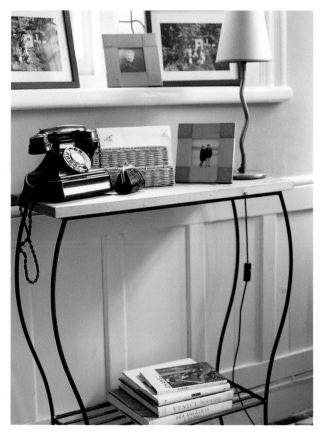

▲ Panelling kits from do-it-yourself stores are an easy way to add character to walls. As an alternative, fit wooden battening to the wall and paint it.

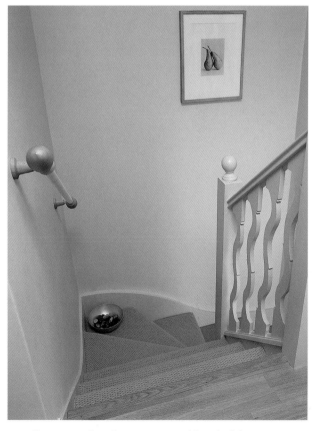

▲ Use a curtain rail as an unusual handrail for extra support down the stairs.

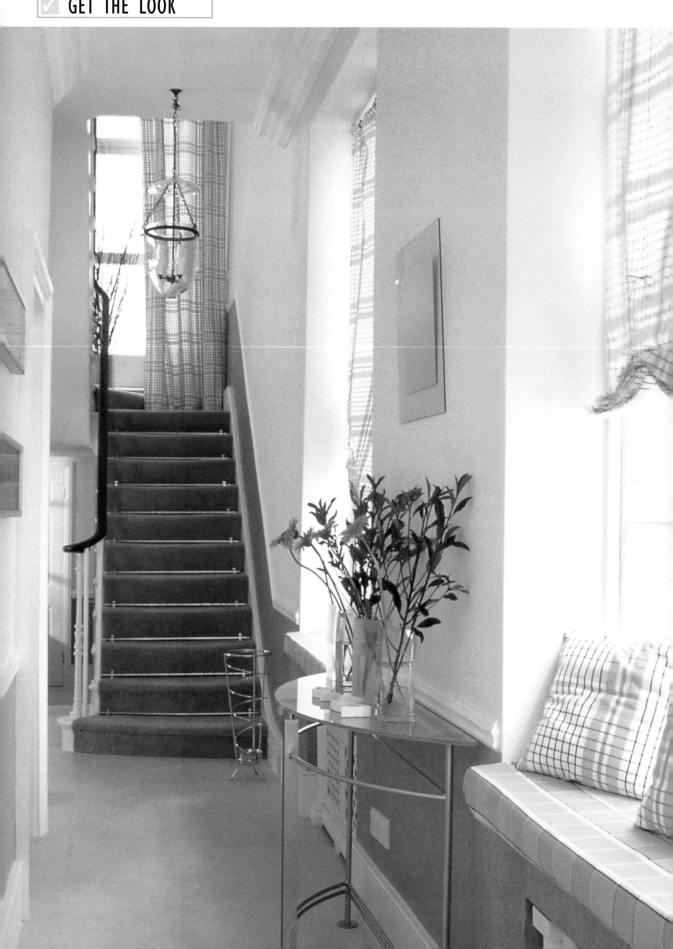

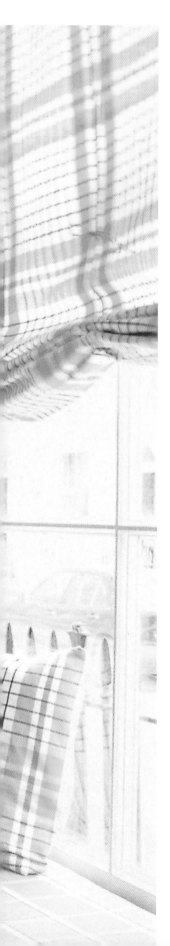

# Warm and welcoming

## Mix warm oranges and golds for a truly inviting hallway.

This hallway manages to be welcoming, functional and interesting all at once. To break up tall walls, divide with a dado rail, painting the lower section in a deep, almost brick red teamed with soft apricot above.

In a long, straight hallway, create points of interest along the way to prevent the eye going straight to the stairs. The semi-circle table takes up virtually no room but acts as a 'punctuation point' and gives you somewhere to display flowers, stack post or drop the car keys.

Turn the windows into focal points by dressing them in jaunty yellow and orange checks. Smart roman blinds are ideal for a hallway, since they are softer than roller blinds but not as fussy as curtains in a confined space.

Pick a carpet with a good, dense quality, which feels luxurious but will wear well. Caramel brown is an ideal colour since it will be forgiving of dirt but doesn't close in the space.

### What else would work?

- suede-effect walls
- accents of olive green
- gilt-framed pictures
- velvet seat cushions

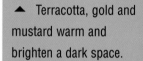

▲ Terracotta, gold and mustard warm and brighten a dark space.

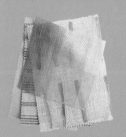

▲ Mix checks and stripes by sticking to the same colour palette.

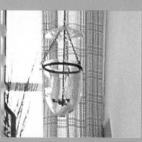

▲ A glowing pendant light acts like a beacon and provides good lighting for the stairs.

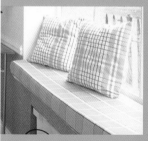

▲ Turn a deep sill into a feature with a seat cushion.

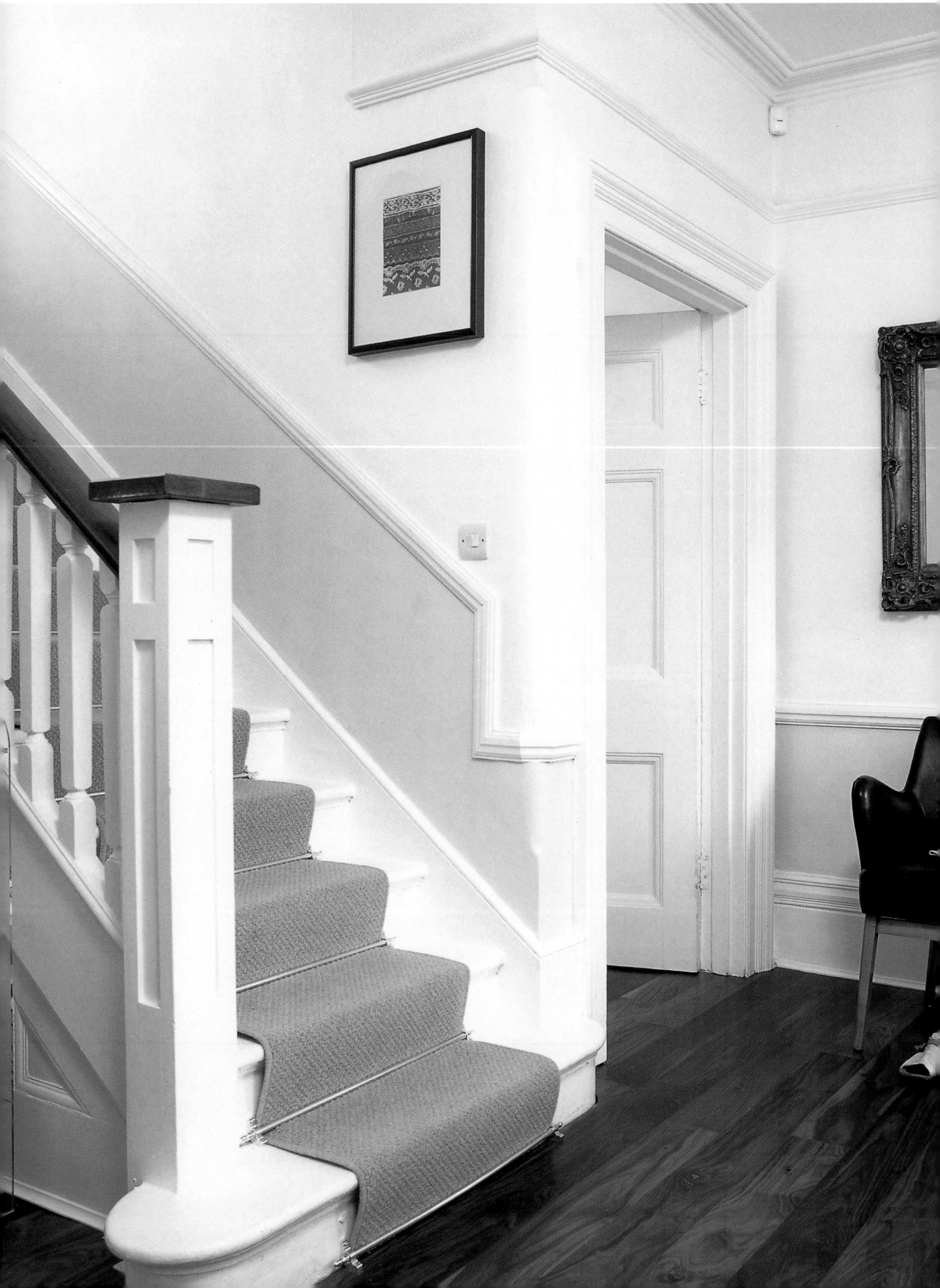

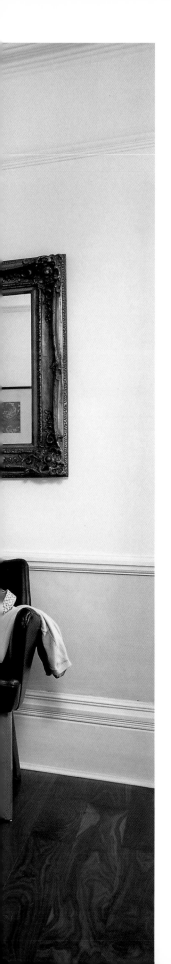

# A grand entrance

## Make the most of a spacious hallway with cool sage and natural textures.

Bigger halls can be a problem – all that space but what to do with it? One answer is to create a period-style entrance hall, complete with grand staircase, dado rail and panelled doors.

Where there is light and space, you can make the floor a feature – here it has been stripped and stained to look like polished mahogany. Pure white woodwork is a classic choice. Use it to increase the sense of space and to frame the stair runner.

Fit a dado rail to divide the wall and provide a natural place for a soft green accent colour, which leads up the stairway. In a tall room, try painting the ceiling in the same accent colour that you use under the dado rail to bring the room together. Place pictures and mirrors to provide focal points; if you can fit one in, a chair is an invaluable addition to any hallway.

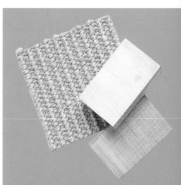

▲ Natural floorcoverings are perfect for hallways. They are tough and there is plenty of colour choice – from dark straw to green and even red.

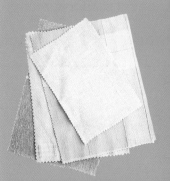

▲ Use textured natural fabrics like linen and hessian for chair seats and window dressings.

### What else would work?

• duck egg blue beneath the dado rail
• sisal floorcovering
• pictures in dark wood frames
• rug in tapestry colours

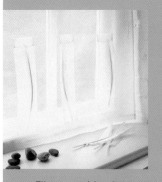

▲ Filter sunshine into your hall with a voile panel. Add an individual touch by sewing slim panels to the lower edge and placing a single feather in each.

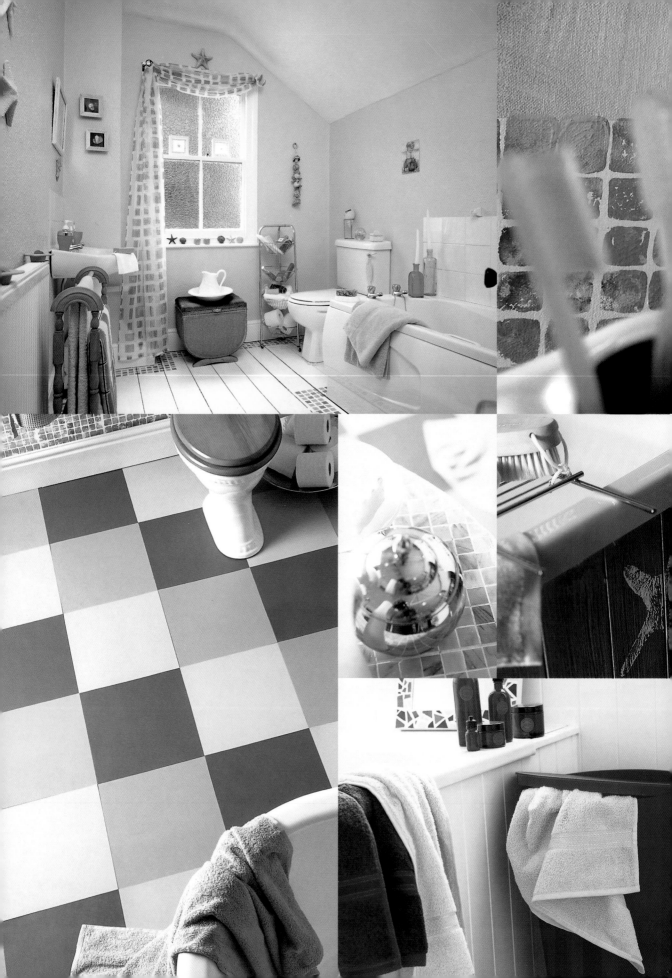

# Bathroom

Most of us have to combine the workaday aspects of bathroom ablutions with the sensual relaxations of the bath to create a room that works on an everyday practical level, but also satisfies the soul on the rare occasions that you can sit back and soak.

   Since the layout of your bathroom furniture and the choice of surfaces are dictated by size, plumbing and practicality, use colour to transform the room from a merely practical space to an enjoyable one. Be bold with colour and clever with space and your bathroom will become one of your favourite rooms in the house.

# Pretty panel blind

This decorative yet practical blind gives you privacy without cutting down on the light that comes into your bathroom. Made from acetate sheets, it's waterproof too.

**1** Measure the window area you want to cover. Using these measurements, work out how many small square, or rectangular, acetate panels will be required for the blind, making sure that each panel is large enough for the motif you have chosen, and allowing for a 5mm (³⁄₁₆in) gap between panels.

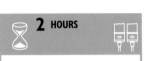

⧖ **2 HOURS**

### You will need
- tape measure
- scissors
- sheets of acetate
- remnant of fabric with a bold floral motif
- self-adhesive clear film
- stationery hole punch
- fine beading wire (available from craft shops)
- fine ribbon

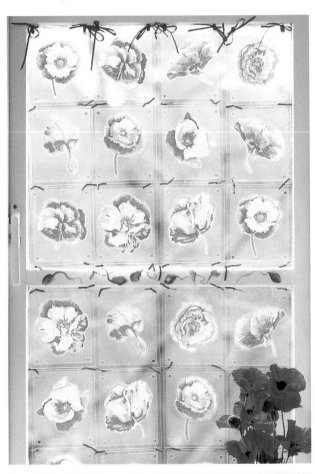

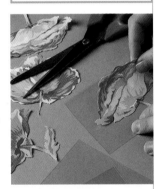

**2** Cut the acetate into the required number of panels, then carefully cut out one floral fabric motif for each panel. Centre a motif on each panel of acetate.

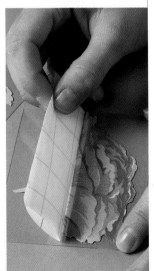

**3** Cut out squares or rectangles of self-adhesive clear film, 5mm (³⁄₁₆in) smaller all round than the acetate. Working on one panel at a time, peel off the backing paper and place the film over the motif to hold it in place.

**4** When all the panels are complete, punch a hole in each corner and tie the panels together with the beading wire. Cut the ribbon into 3cm (1¼in) lengths and tie around the beading wire to decorate.

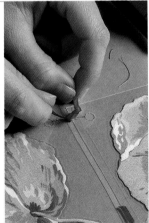

# Wallpaper border frames

Get imaginative with wallpaper borders and create panels and inset details to add interest to your wall. The effect can be as simple or elaborate as you choose – from a single panel to a whole wall.

**1** To make a 'frame' using a wallpaper border paper, mark out the area on the wall to be framed using a pencil and ruler. Check that your lines are straight with a spirit level. Paste a horizontal strip top and bottom, with their edges butting up to your pencil line. Smooth over with the wallpaper brush to ensure that there are no air bubbles.

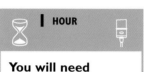

**HOUR**

### You will need
- pencil and ruler
- spirit level
- vinyl wallpaper border
- vinyl wallpaper paste and brush
- sharp knife

**2** Paste the vertical pieces in the same way, overlapping the horizontal pieces at the corners. At each corner, mitre the overlapping border strips by taking a sharp knife and cutting through both layers of border on a diagonal line from the inside corner of the frame to the outer corner. Peel away the offcuts and brush the border back into place.

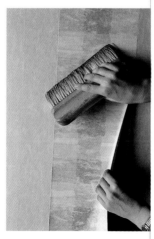

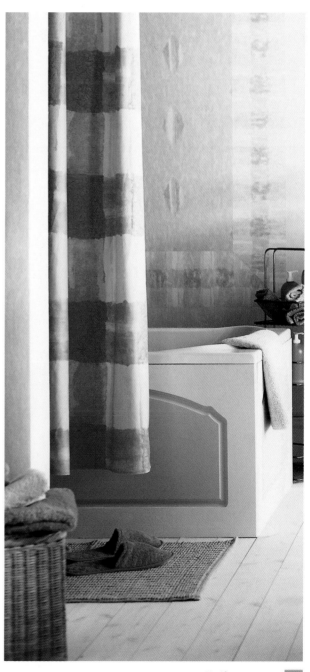

# Distressed wood panelling

Give your bath panel a rustic distressed effect with this shortcut technique. The effect works best on wood with detail and edges, such as tongue and groove panelling.

⏳ **2 HOURS**
**plus drying**

**You will need**
- oil-based paint in two contrasting colours
- household paintbrushes
- petroleum jelly
- clean cloth

**1** Paint your bath panel in your base coat, in this case red, and leave to dry. Take a small paintbrush, dip it into the petroleum jelly and apply it randomly to the edges, moulding and joins, with random smears towards the top and bottom of the panel, where wear and tear would naturally occur.

**2** Apply the top coat of paint, in this case blue, over the wood and petroleum jelly. Leave paint to dry thoroughly.

**3** Using a clean cloth, gently rub off the jelly, following the direction of the grain. The areas where the jelly was applied will have prevented the top coat adhering and will rub off to reveal the bottom coat of paint, creating a distressed effect.

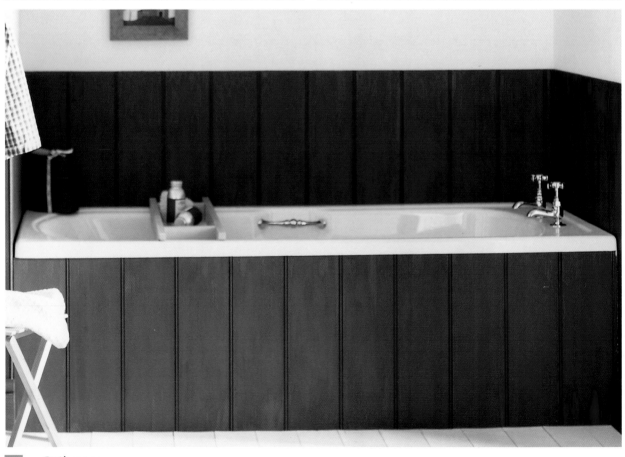

# Painted floor rug

Give bare floorboards instant impact by creating a stunning design like this 'Stars and Stripes'. Paint it in front of the bath, like a rug, or position it so that it welcomes you into the room as you open the door.

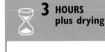

**3 HOURS**
plus drying

**You will need**
- oil-based paint in white, blue and red
- household paintbrushes
- pencil and low-tack masking tape
- felt-tip pen
- piece of sponge
- scalpel
- old plate
- scrap paper

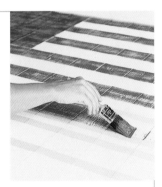

**1** Prepare the floorboards by ensuring that they are clean, dry and smooth. Paint the whole floor in white and leave to dry. Mark out the design lightly on the boards, then mask off the areas for the different colours. Start by painting the blue area and leave to dry thoroughly before remasking and painting the red stripes. Don't overload the brush with paint each time. Use it almost dry and build up the colour so that the result is a little patchy, giving a slightly worn look rather than solid colour.

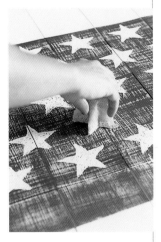

**2** For the stars, make a stamp from a sponge. Draw a star shape on the sponge with a felt-tip pen and cut out the shape using a scalpel. Pour a little of the white paint on to a plate and dip the sponge into the paint. Practise stamping stars on a spare sheet of paper until you get the hang of the amount of paint and pressure you need to use, then press stars on to the flag and leave to dry.

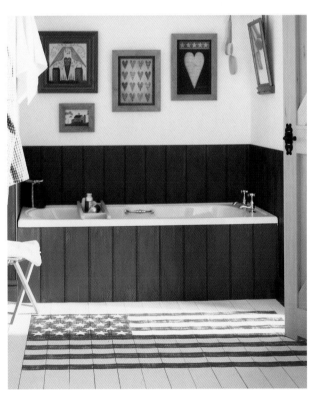

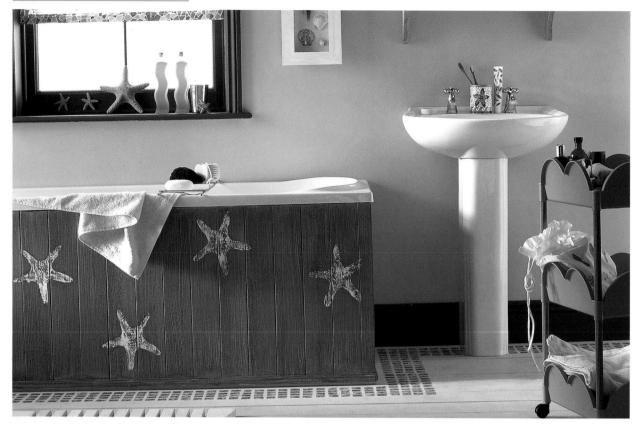

# Starfish bath panel

Created using a reverse stamping technique, this starfish is a great touch for a seaside-themed bathroom.

**2 HOURS**
plus drying

**You will need**
- woodwash in white
- household paintbrush
- pencil and card
- scissors
- piece of foam
- craft knife
- masking fluid
- rag
- emulsion paint in blue
- cloth or sponge

**1** Paint the bath panel with a couple of coats of white woodwash, allowing the first coat to dry before applying the second.

**2** Make a starfish template by drawing a starfish shape on to a piece of card. Place the template on a piece of foam and cut out with a craft knife.

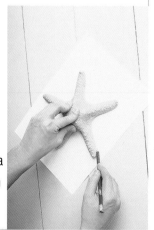

**3** Pour masking fluid on to a rag and transfer to the foam starfish. Press the foam shape on to the bath panel in a random pattern.

**4** Dilute the blue emulsion paint with one-third water and paint on to the bath panel. Leave to dry, then use a cloth or sponge to rub off the masking fluid so that the starfish pattern shows through.

# Frosted bathroom cabinet

Make your own roomy bathroom cabinet from the carcass of an old chest of drawers and add frosted doors for a contemporary look. Finish it with paint or woodstain to match your bathroom.

**1** Shake the woodwash well and apply two coats to the chest, inside and out, allowing the first coat to dry before applying the second coat.

**2** Measure the front of the chest. Using a scalpel and metal ruler, cut two pieces of polypropylene the same height as the chest and half the width to make two vertical doors.

**3** Using a handsaw, cut eight wooden battens to make the door frames. Cut four battens the same height as the doors, and four battens to fit across the width of the doors, inside the upright battens. Apply two coats of woodwash to the battens and leave to dry.

**4** Apply glue to the battens and press them around the edges of each polypropylene door. Leave to dry for at least two hours before attaching the doors to the chest using two butt hinges for each door. Drill a hole along the top edge of each door for the aluminium knobs and fix in place.

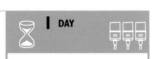

**DAY**

### You will need

- woodwash
- household paintbrush
- wooden chest with drawers removed
- tape measure and pencil
- scalpel and metal ruler
- sheet of polypropylene
- handsaw
- wooden battening
- strong glue
- 4 butt hinges
- electric drill
- 2 small aluminium knobs

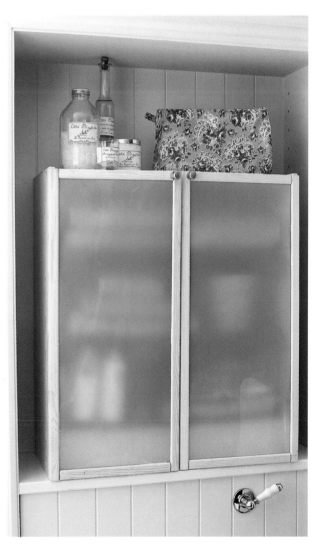

# All squared up

## Jazzy tiled floor

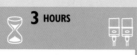

- Work out your design on paper first – try random, chequered or striped designs or borders of colour – then roughly lay out the tiles on the floor to see where you need to make cuts and adjustments. Try to centre the design in the room so that you will have equal amounts of cut tiles bordering the room. Do this by drawing horizontal and vertical lines across the floor so that they cross in the centre of the room, then work outwards from this point. Lay all the whole tiles first and cut the rest to fit as necessary.

**3 HOURS**

**You will need**
- pencil and paper
- self-adhesive floor tiles in two or three colours
- sharp decorating knife
- tape measure

## Mosaic-topped table

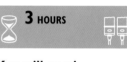

- Spread tile adhesive over the table top and lay mosaic sheets on top, face down if they are the paper-backed kind, face up if they are mesh-backed mosaics. Fill the gaps with single tiles snipped out of the sheet and cut to shape with the tile nibbler. Leave to dry before grouting. Finish by sponging the top clean.

**3 HOURS**

**You will need**
- tile adhesive
- old table
- sheets of mosaic tiles
- tile nibbler
- grout and sponge

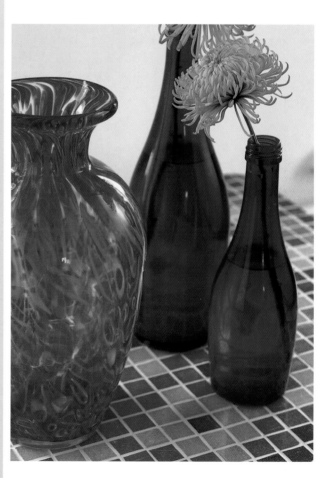

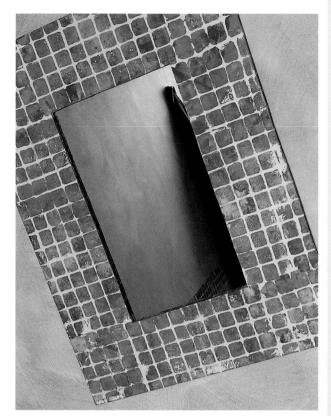

# Fake mosaic stamp

- Mark the foam into 2cm (¾in) squares using a pencil and ruler. Cut away along the lines with a scalpel to form 'grout' lines without cutting all the way through. Paint a border of white around the wall and leave to dry.

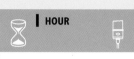

**I HOUR**

## You will need
- piece of compacted foam rubber
- pencil, ruler and scalpel
- small household paintbrush
- emulsion paint in white, plus three shades of blue
- piece of board to use as 'palette'
- kitchen paper

- Blend all three blue paints together lightly on your palette. Dip the foam stamp into the mixed paint, remove excess paint by pressing on to kitchen paper, then press the foam firmly against the wall and remove carefully. Repeat all the way along the border.

# Mosaic-stamped mirror

- Wearing a dust mask, use a jigsaw to cut out the centre of the piece of MDF to leave a 'hole' just slightly smaller than your mirror tile. Prime the MDF frame all over. When dry, paint the frame front and edges with white emulsion paint and leave to dry.

**I HOUR**
**plus drying**

## You will need
- dust mask and jigsaw
- rectangle or square of 12mm (½in) MDF, 10cm (4in) wider and longer than the mirror tile
- rectangular or square mirror tile
- MDF primer
- household paintbrushes
- emulsion paint in white, plus one other colour
- mosaic stamp
- clear matt varnish
- heavy-duty sticky tape

- Stamp the frame with a mosaic stamp using the darker colour of paint. When the paint is dry, apply a coat of varnish. To finish, tape the mirror into position on the back of the frame using heavy-duty sticky tape.

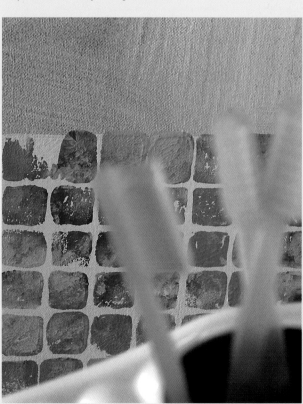

# Clever bathroom tricks

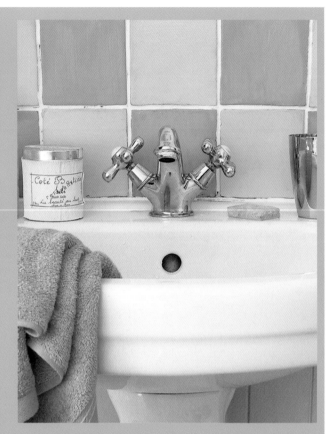

## Bamboo towel rail

• Cut six bamboo canes to the desired height of the finished towel rail. Using twine at the top and the bottom, tie them together in threes to make the two uprights of the towel rail.

**30 MINUTES**

**You will need**
• hacksaw
• 7 x 3m (3¼yd) long bamboo canes
• twine

Lay them on the floor so that the tops of the struts are 8.5cm (3¼in) apart and the bottoms are 40cm (16in) apart. Check that this will give you enough space on which to hang your towels, and work out how many rungs you want and where they will go.

From the remaining bamboo cane, cut each rung to fit, overlapping each upright by 2.5cm (1in). Secure the rungs to the uprights with twine and lean the finished rail against a wall.

## Revamped tiled splashback

• Prepare the existing tiles with primer according to the manufacturer's instructions. When dry, paint over them with tile paint in alternate colours to get a chequered design. When dry, run the grout pen over the original grout to give it a cleaner, whiter finish.

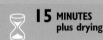

**15 MINUTES**
**plus drying**

**You will need**
• tile primer
• small household paintbrush
• tile paint in two colours
• grout pen

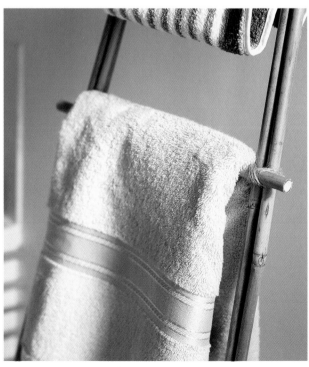

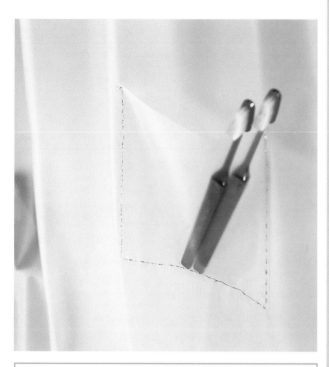

## Mini wall storage

- Decide where you want your containers to go. Then, using a pencil and spirit level, mark where the top edge of each container will be. Mark on the back of each container where the screws will go and carefully

**15 MINUTES** per container

**You will need**
- wooden or plastic boxes
- pencil and spirit level
- screwdriver and screws
- electric drill and wallplugs

drill holes for the screws. Working with one container at a time, hold the container to the line on the wall and drill through the screw holes into the wall. Remove the container, insert wallplugs, then screw the container to the wall. You could apply lettering to the front of the boxes using transfers or acrylic paint.

## Shower curtain pockets

- This panel clips to the front of your shower curtain and is just one-third the full width of the shower curtain so that it hangs neatly when drawn back. Cut the clear plastic sheeting to size, 5cm (2in) longer than the shower curtain and one-third of its

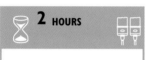

**2 HOURS**

**You will need**
- tape measure
- scissors
- clear plastic sheeting
- plain shower curtain
- needle and silver thread

width. Sew a 5cm (2in) hem at one end of the panel using silver thread – this will be the top of the panel.

- Cut out small pockets from the remaining plastic sheeting and sew them on to the panel, stitching around three sides but leaving the top edges open. Fill the pockets with decorative flower heads and leaves and colourful bathroom bits such as toothbrushes. Punch eyelets through the hemmed edge and hang the panel from the shower curtain clips nearest to the wall.

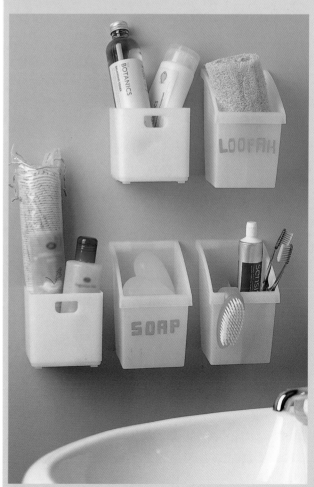

# A dash of pebbles

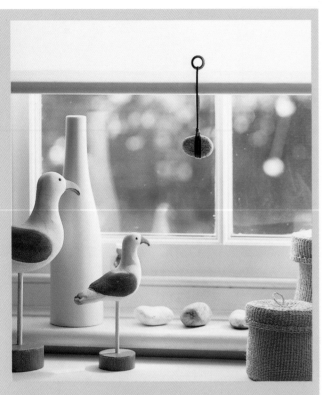

## Bathroom candle pots

• Wash the pots in warm soapy water to ensure that they are clean and leave to dry completely. Paint the pots inside and out with emulsion paint. When dry, half fill with stones, stand a candle in the centre and push more stones around the candle to hold it in place.

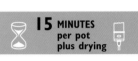

⏳ **15** MINUTES per pot plus drying 🖌

**You will need**
• terracotta pots
• emulsion paint
• household paintbrush
• small stones
• stout candles

## Pebble blind pull

• Snip the existing pull neatly off the blind. Using the eyelet punch, make a hole in the centre of the blind 7cm (2¾in) from the bottom edge. Wrap the leather thong two or three times around the pebble and knot tightly to secure. Thread the ends of the leather through the eyelet hole and tie to secure, with the knot tucked out of sight on the window side of the blind. Trim the excess thong.

⏳ **10** MINUTES 🖌

**You will need**
• scissors
• plain blind
• eyelets and eyelet punch
• tape measure
• length of leather thong
• pebble

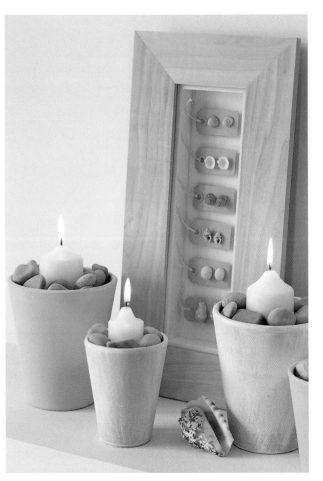

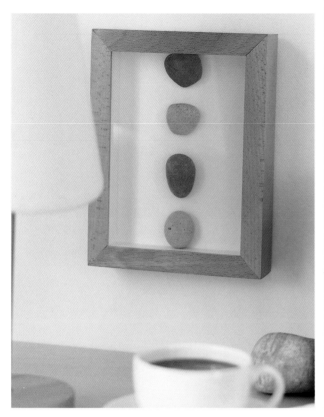

# Striped bamboo blind

• Make sure you are in a well-ventilated room or even outdoors. Unroll the blind completely and lay flat on plenty of newspaper or plastic sheeting. Work out the width and spacing you want for your stripes to be and mark them out along the length of the blind. Tape newspaper either side of each stripe to cover completely and protect the areas which will not be sprayed. Hold the can six inches away from the blind and spray on the stripes. Spray evenly and lightly, building up the colour gradually. Leave to dry. For the best effect, turn the blind over and spray matching stripes on the back.

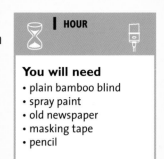

I HOUR

**You will need**
• plain bamboo blind
• spray paint
• old newspaper
• masking tape
• pencil

# Pebble box frame

• Cut the card to fit in the box frame. Position the pebbles on the card, and when you are happy with the arrangement, fix a sticky pad to the back of each pebble and press on to the card. Attach the card to the frame backing with more sticky pads, then insert the card into the frame.

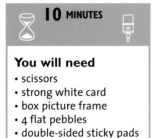

I0 MINUTES

**You will need**
• scissors
• strong white card
• box picture frame
• 4 flat pebbles
• double-sided sticky pads

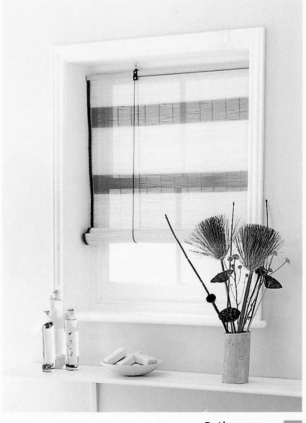

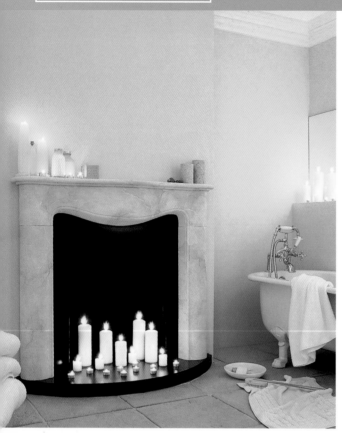

# Shades of warmth

Warm the room with spicy oranges and rich wood tones for an inviting bathroom retreat, far removed from the austere cold white of some bathrooms.

▲ Enjoy long, soothing candlelit baths. Generous quantities of candles will transform any bathroom into a romantic retreat.

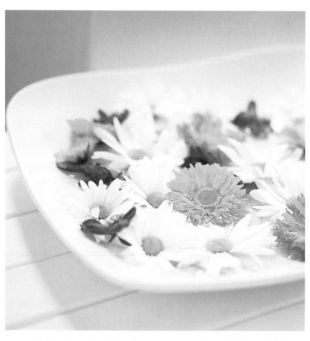

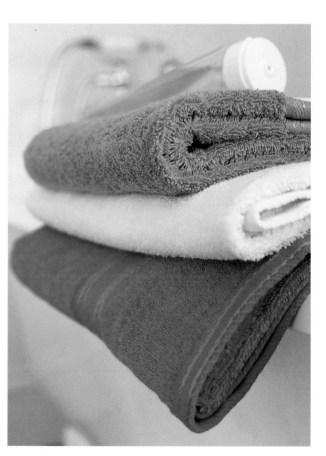

▲ Add a touch of freshness and colour with a shallow dish filled with water in which to float little flower heads.

▲ Bring your bathroom to life with towels in vibrant, toning colours.

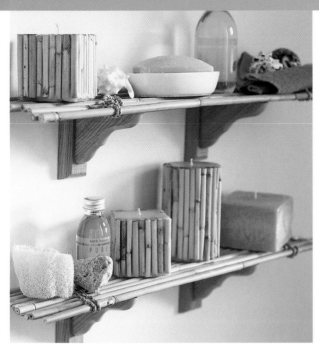

▲ Make instant shelves for your bathroom with lengths of bamboo cane cut to size and lashed together with twine. Balance on sturdy brackets fixed to the wall.

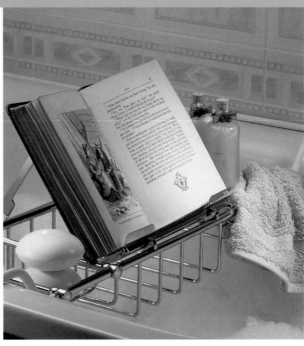

▲ For leisurely bathing – and to save your favourite read from damp, wrinkly pages – clip a book holder to your bath rack.

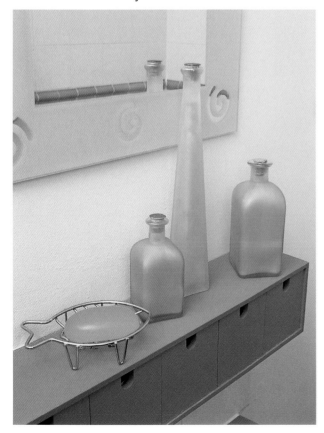

▲ Use mini storage boxes screwed to the wall as a handy narrow shelf. Coat with gloss paint to protect from damp and spills.

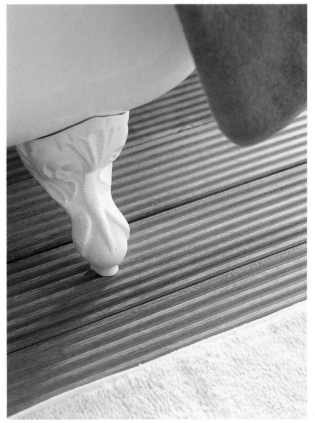

▲ For a really unusual, yet practical, floor covering, try outdoor decking. It works brilliantly in a bathroom since it is designed to be waterproof.

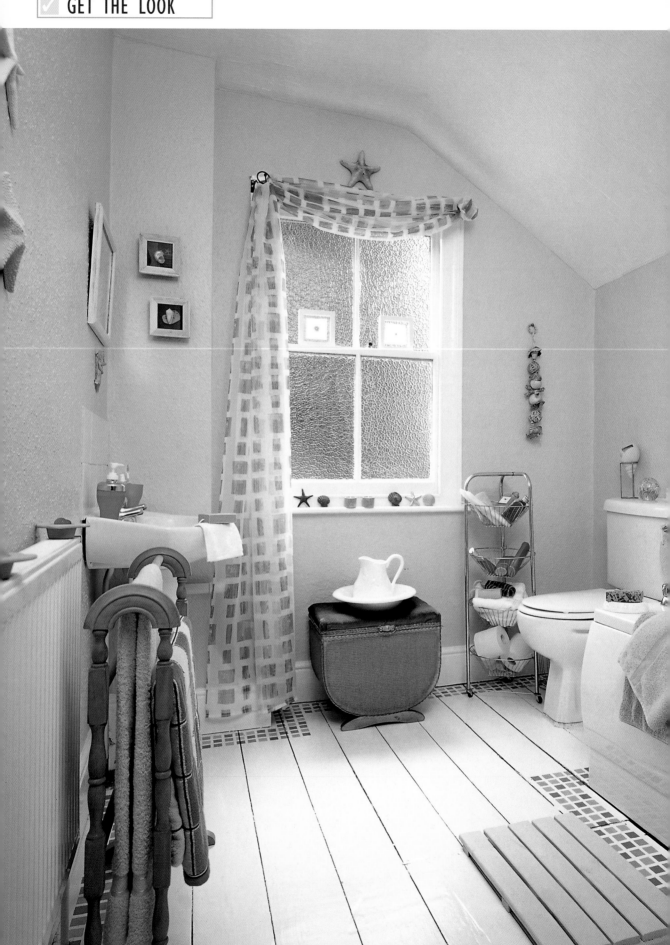

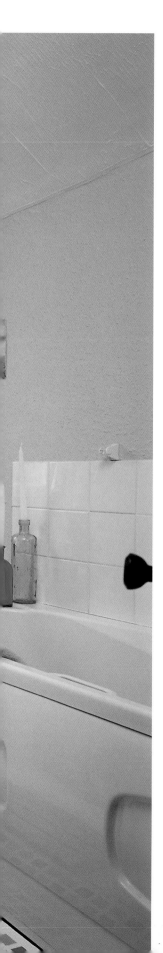

# Touch of the seashore

Revel in a bathroom inspired by the ocean blue of tropical seas and collections of beach treasures.

Think silver sands and azure seas to get the feel of this bathroom. Blue can look cold, especially in bathrooms that receive little natural light like this one. Use a soft, pale sea green on the walls to make the room look spacious and airy, yet warm and inviting at the same time.

For a bargain alternative to expensive floorcoverings, rip up the carpet and paint the floorboards with white gloss or a water-resistant stain to open up the floor space. Use a border of fake mosaic tiles to define the space and draw the eye downwards rather than up towards the high ceiling.

Bring touches of azure blue and turquoise into the bathroom with accessories that add interest. Finish the room with seashore finds – shells and starfish, old bottles and driftwood picture frames.

### What else would work?

- luxurious white towels
- chrome towel rail
- aqua tiles inset into the bath and basin surrounds
- roller blind stamped with mosaic or shell motif

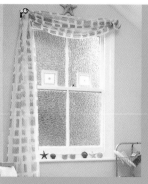

▲ Take a generous length of voile and drape it across the top of the window frame, hanging down one side to add a bit of drama.

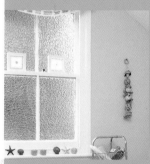

▲ Use shells gathered on a piece of rough twine, framed singly in wooden box frames or arranged along a windowsill.

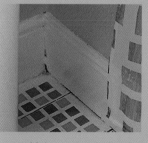

▲ Make a mosaic border by cutting nine squares out of a sheet of stencil card. Tape to the floor and stencil using shades of blue and green.

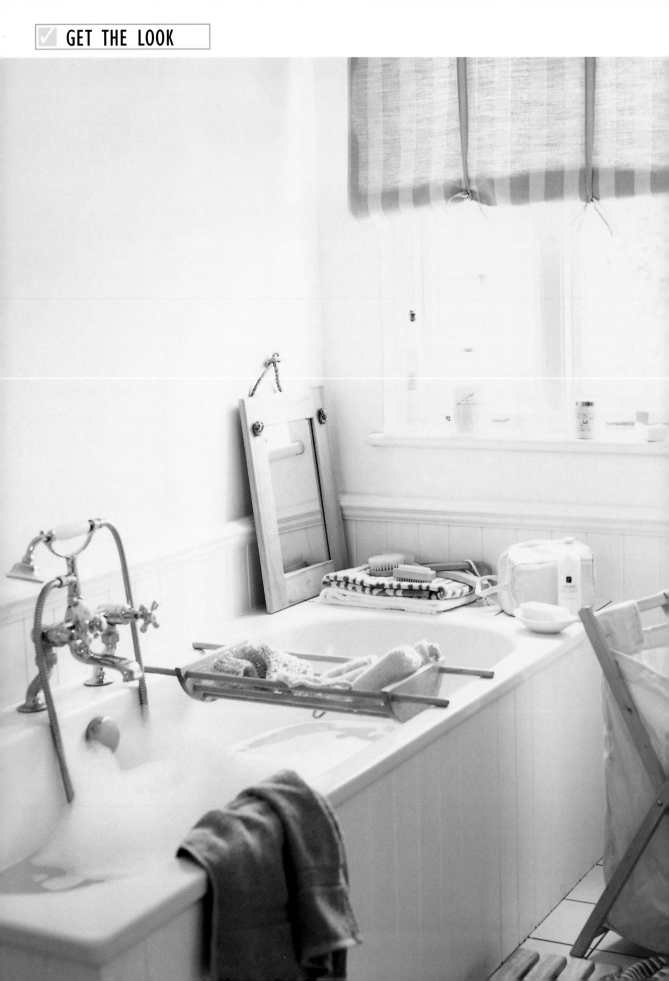

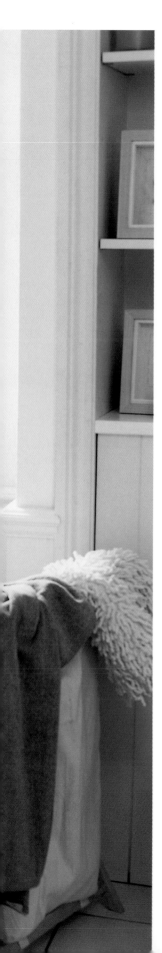

# Chocolate, cream and cocoa

## Bring warmth to a small bathroom by using layers of neutral shades.

Keep the wall, floor and suite all white to give a tiny room a feeling of light and space. Choose a slightly off-white shade to give that soft, diffused feel, rather than brilliant white, which can look clinical. Paint all the woodwork and panelling in white as well to make it look bigger, without losing the interest that the texture and detail give to the room.

Next, choose both accessories and necessities to add layers of natural colours: towels in rich brown, cream and sand, a canvas laundry holder, unfinished woods (wax them to make them more moisture resistant), and a simple reef blind in striped linen. Choose materials that have plenty of natural texture to complete a room that is irresistibly touchable.

### What else would work?

- hints of olive green
- white shutters at the window
- whitewashed floorboards
- a row of cacti in stone pots on the windowsill

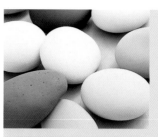

▲ Think edible shades – chocolate, cream, eggshell and dark cocoa.

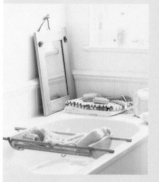

▲ Look for interesting textures, like a plaited rope to hang a pine mirror, wooden body brushes and loofahs.

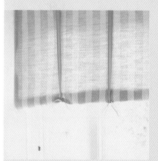

▲ Make a simple blind by hemming a piece of fabric slightly wider and longer than the window and fixing eyelets along the top to hang from chrome hooks above the window. Roll up the blind and hold in place with two lengths of ribbon hung either side.

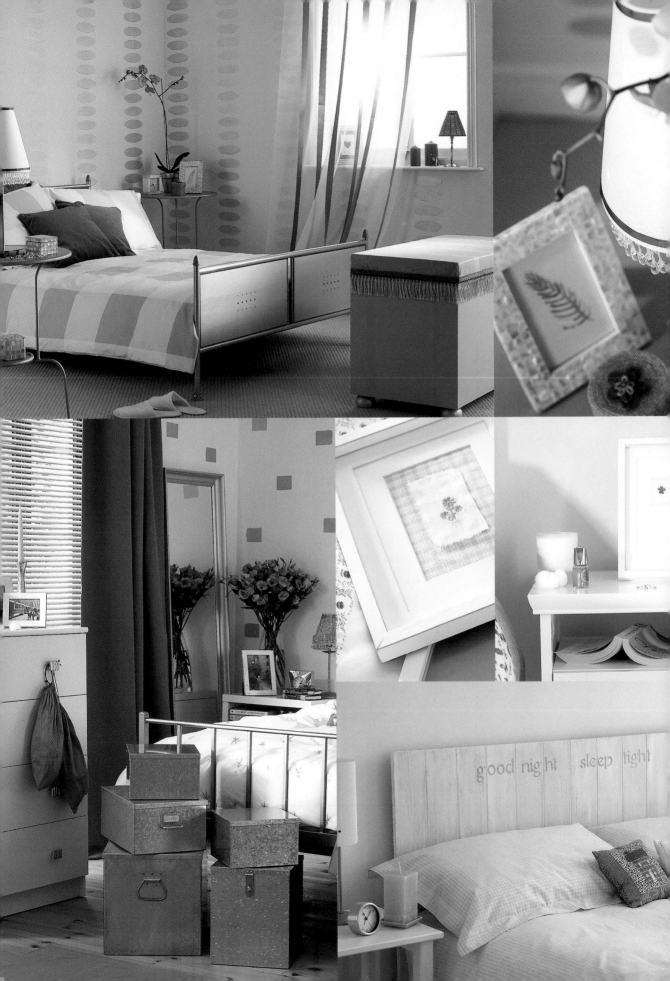

good night sleep tight

# Bedroom

This is your private space, the room least seen by the outside world and the one where you can indulge your senses. Think carefully about what you need your bedroom to be – relaxing, sensuous or rejuvenating? Is this a space for you alone, you and your partner or for the whole family?

Whether you want your bedroom to be a place that relaxes you in the evening or lifts your mood when you open your eyes in the morning, colour is the key to creating the most personal, fantasy-fulfilling space.

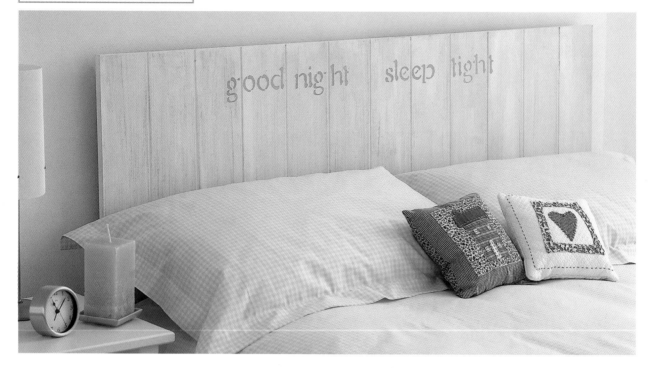

# Shaker-style headboard

A simple piece of MDF is transformed with routed grooves
and paint into a panelled headboard stencilled with lettering.
It stands on batten legs behind the bed.

**4 HOURS**
per wall
plus drying

## You will need
- tape measure and pencil
- dust mask
- sheet of 12mm (½in) MDF
- 2 wooden battens
- G-clamps
- blocks of wood
- electric router
- MDF primer
- household paintbrushes
- oil-based paint in two colours
- lettering stencil
- electric drill
- screwdriver and screws

**1** Work out the required size of your headboard – usually 3cm (1¼in) wider than your bed and standing 40–60cm (16–24in) above the mattress. Wearing a dust mask, cut the MDF to these dimensions. Cut the battens to reach from the floor to 10cm (4in) below the top of the headboard.

**2** Decide on the spacing of the grooves for the tongue and groove panelling effect, making sure they are spaced evenly across the width of the headboard. Measure and mark the top and bottom of the

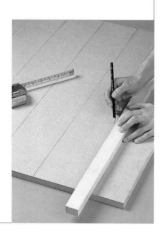

piece of MDF with a pencil, then join the marks to make lines.

**3** Clamp the MDF to a worksurface with G-clamps, placing a piece of wood under each clamp to protect the MDF and to use as a guide for the router. Rout along the pencil lines to a depth of 3mm (⅛in).

**4** Prime the headboard. When dry, apply a coat of oil-based paint and leave to

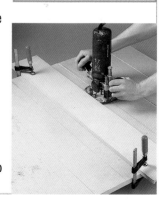

dry. Stencil your lettering across the headboard in a contrasting colour.

**5** When the paint is dry, turn the headboard face down. On the back of the

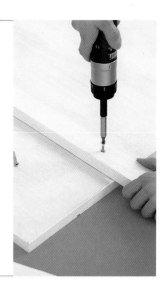

board, make a pencil mark along the bottom edge of the headboard, 20cm (8in) in from one side edge. Make another mark halfway up the headboard, again 20cm (8in) in from the side edge. Position one batten against

these marks and drill then screw into place. Fix the other batten in the same way at the other end of the headboard. To finish, stand the headboard against the wall and push the bed against it to hold it in place.

# Decorated linen box

Turn an inexpensive box into the perfect piece of bedroom furniture by painting then finishing it with a pretty stamped motif.

**1** Paint the box with white emulsion and leave to dry. Pour some blue paint into a saucer, then roller on to the flower stamp.

**2** Stamp flowers in a border pattern all around the chest lid and up the sides. Seal the paintwork with a coat of acrylic varnish all over.

**2 HOURS** plus drying

**You will need**
- bare pine box, primed if necessary
- emulsion paint in white and blue
- household paintbrushes
- flower and stamp
- old saucer
- small roller
- acrylic varnish

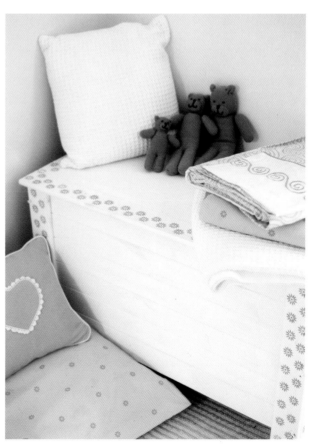

# Sponged checked walls

Re-create the look of expensive designer wallpaper using masking tape, paint and a cloth to sponge on rows of squares for an eye-catching yet subtle effect.

**3 HOURS**
per wall
plus drying

**You will need**
- emulsion paint in two colours
- large household paintbrush
- tape measure and pencil
- scissors and low-tack masking tape
- paint tray
- clean, lint-free cloth

**1** Paint the entire wall in the base colour and leave to dry thorougly.

**2** Using a tape measure and pencil, mark out the position of the 'tiles' on the wall. Cut lengths of masking tape and trim the edges randomly to create uneven lines and achieve a hand-painted look. Leaving the tape untrimmed will give a more formal effect. Stick the masking tape along the marked pencil lines to create masked-off squares.

**3** Decant some of the paint for the top coat into a paint tray. Screw up the cloth and dip it into the paint. Gently dab the cloth over the masked squares. When the paint is dry, carefully peel away the masking tape. Rub out pencil marks.

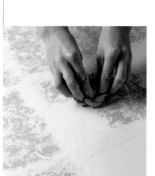

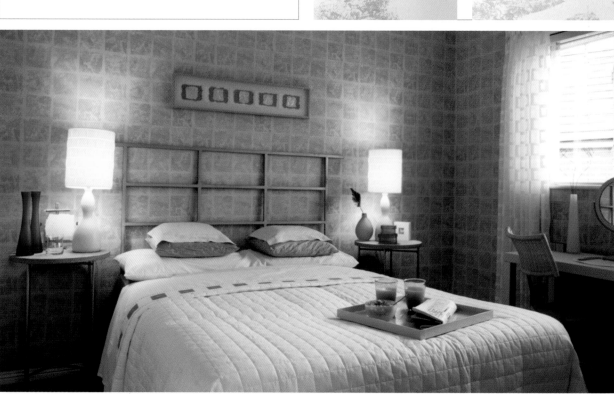

# Bedside shelf

No room for a bedside table for your morning cup of tea? This stylish stacked shelf, made with lengths of sturdy pine board stacked together, is the answer.

**1** You need to saw the plank into eight lengths. Start by marking out the lengths so as to plan the best use of your plank. The longest should be 50cm (20in) long and use the full width of the plank. Each successive board should be 4cm (1½in) shorter and 1cm (⅜in) narrower. Using a circular saw, cut out the eight lengths.

**2** Sand any rough edges. Stack the pieces with the longest at the bottom, best face down, so that each piece is centred evenly on the one below but lined up along one edge. You should end up with one tiered edge and one straight edge, which will sit against the wall. Mark where each piece of wood will sit on the one below. Apply wood glue to the largest board, then place the next piece on top, using the pencil marks as a guide.

**3** Secure with three nails at each end (the smaller boards will need only two). Make sure the nails are hidden by the next board. Continue attaching the boards in the same way, but don't nail the last one. Let the glue dry.

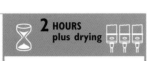

### You will need
- 18 x 288cm (7 x 113in) length of 1.5cm (⅝) pine board
- pencil and tape measure
- circular saw
- sandpaper
- wood glue
- hammer and 4cm (1½in) nails
- primer
- household paintbrushes
- emulsion or oil-based paint
- screwdriver and screws
- 2 keyhole washers
- spirit level
- electric drill and wallplugs

**2 HOURS** plus drying

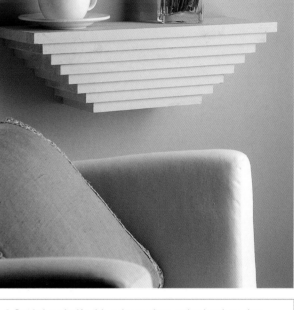

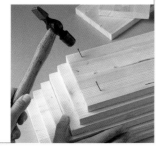

**4** Seal the shelf with primer, then paint it when dry. Attach two keyhole washers to the back of the shelf, 40cm (16in) apart. Hold the shelf against the wall and use a spirit level to ensure that it is straight. Mark then drill holes in the wall, insert wallplugs and screw the shelf on to the wall.

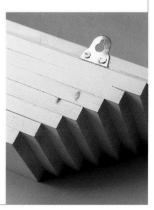

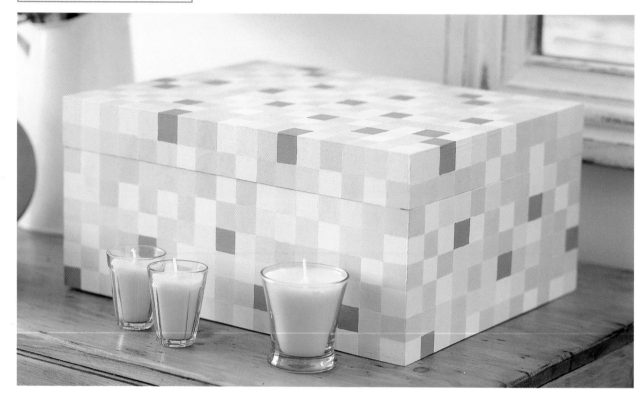

# Mosaic-look keepsake box

Turn an old wooden box into something special by painting it in a rainbow of colours of your choosing. It's a great way to use up leftover paint or you could buy a handful of tester pots.

⧗ **3 HOURS** per wall plus drying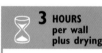

**You will need**
- wooden box
- pencil and ruler
- small square-edged artist's paintbrush
- vinyl matt emulsion paint in six to eight different colours
- small household brush
- clear matt acrylic varnish

**1** Measure your box, including the sides of the lid, and calculate how the dimensions divide equally into squares – the ones here are 2cm (¾in) squares.

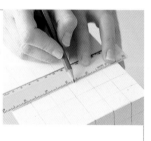

Using a pencil and ruler, draw horizontal then vertical lines to divide the surfaces of the box into squares.

**2** Using a square-edged artist's brush and working with one colour at a time, paint the squares in a

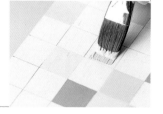

random pattern. Make sure each set of squares is dry before you begin painting the next colour.

**3** Allow the completed box to dry, then check on your finished pattern. If there are too many squares in one colour or the groupings appear uneven, adjust by painting over them in one of the other colours. Finish off by applying two coats of clear varnish.

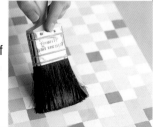

# Reverse stencilling

Here, a stencil is applied in vertical rows across the wall, and flipped on alternate rows for a mirror image effect. You need to choose a stencil that works well when repeated in a vertical line.

**1** Paint the wall with your base colour and leave to dry. Draw two vertical pencil lines on the wall, leaving a 45cm (18in) gap between each line. Place the stencil directly over one of the lines and tape it in place.

**3 HOURS** per wall plus drying

### You will need
- emulsion paint for base colour
- household paintbrush
- pencil and steel rule
- stencil
- low-tack masking tape
- stencil brush
- stencil or emulsion paint in off-white

**2** Load the stencil brush with the off-white paint and stipple over the stencil. Do not put too much paint on the brush – use it almost dry and build up the layers to get the desired effect. Remove the stencil and refix so that the motifs join in a continuous line.

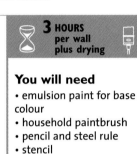

**3** For the second line of stencilling, clean the stencil thoroughly and turn it over so that you are stencilling on the reverse. Line it up over the second pencilled line and repeat the procedure. Continue stencilling the wall in the same way, flipping the stencil for each alternate line.

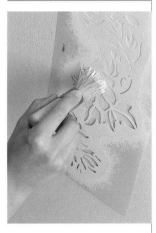

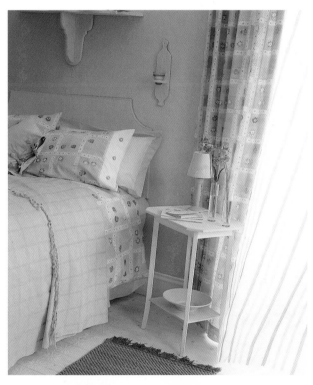

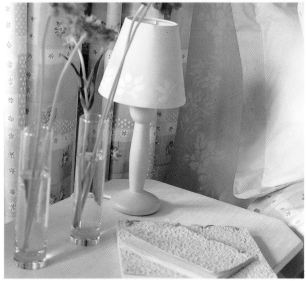

# Checks and flowers

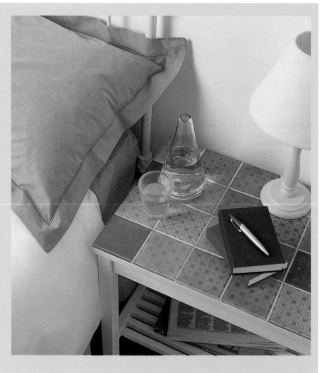

## Patchwork curtain panel

• Measure the width of your window and from track or pole down to where you want the curtain to hang. Cut your fabric into 30cm (12in) squares, allowing 5cm (2in) extra for hemming side pieces and 7.5cm (3in) for hemming pieces along the top and bottom of the curtain panel. Join pieces in rows widthways, press open the seams, then join rows to make the curtain length. Hem all the way round and hang the panel using curtain clips.

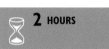

⧗ **2 HOURS**

**You will need**
• tape measure
• scissors
• remnants of patterned fabrics
• sewing machine or needle and thread
• curtain clips
• iron

## Tiled table top

• Measure the table top to work out how many tiles you will need. Position the tiles on the table top. Mark then cut any tiles around the edges of the table top that need to be cut to fit. Sand the table top, wipe it clean of dust, then cover with a layer of tile adhesive. Place the tiles in position, leaving even spaces in between them for the grout. Push firmly in place and leave to dry. Grout the gaps when the tiles are firmly fixed, then sponge away the excess grout.

⧗ **2 HOURS**

**You will need**
• tape measure
• table to be tiled
• tiles and tile cutter
• sandpaper
• tile adhesive
• grout and sponge

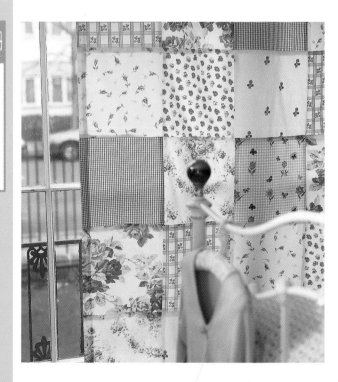

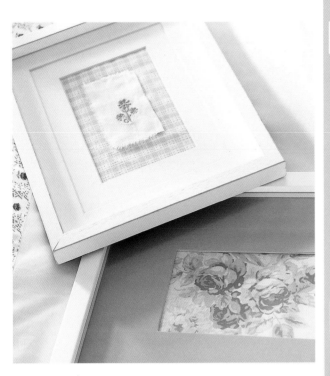

## Wallpaper-panelled furniture

• If the front panel of the cabinet can be removed, do so. Coat it with a thin layer of PVA glue, leave until slightly tacky, then stretch the fabric or smooth wallpaper over the panel. If the panel cannot be removed, simply cut the wallpaper or fabric to fit and fix it in place in the same way.

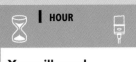

**I HOUR**

**You will need**
• bedside cabinet
• PVA glue
• scissors
• remnant of fabric or wallpaper

## Fabric scrap pictures

• Cut one piece of the card to fit inside the picture frame as a picture mount and another piece on which to mount the fabric. Place the larger piece of fabric on the card as a backdrop and place a scrap of fabric with a floral motif on top and

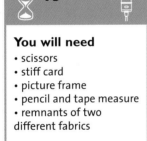

**I 5 MINUTES**

**You will need**
• scissors
• stiff card
• picture frame
• pencil and tape measure
• remnants of two different fabrics

replace in the frame. Re-assemble the picture frame – the glass should hold the fabric in place.

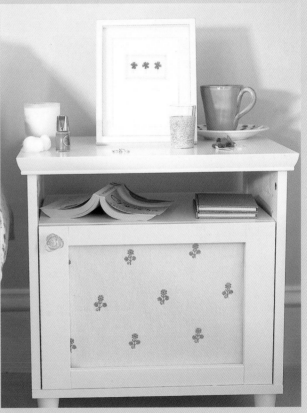

# Silver 'n' pink

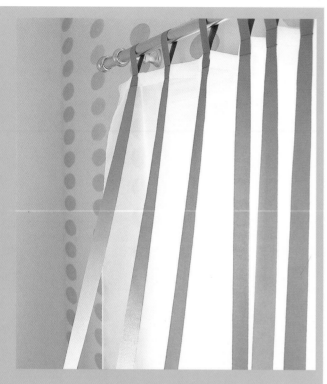

## Crystal-trimmed lampshade

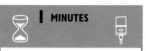

⏳ **1 MINUTES**

**You will need**
- crystal trim
- plain white lampshade
- scissors
- PVA glue
- narrow ribbon

● Wrap the crystal trim around the bottom edge of the lampshade to work out the length needed, then cut to length. Run a thin line of PVA glue around the inside bottom edge of the lampshade and stick the trim to the inside of the shade. Wrap the ribbon around the bottom and top edges of the lampshade, 5mm (³⁄₁₆in) from the edge, to determine the correct length. Cut the ribbon to size, run a thin line of glue around the shade and stick the ribbon down.

## Ribbon tab-top curtain

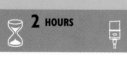

⏳ **2 HOURS**

**You will need**
- scissors
- long length of ribbon
- tape measure
- sheer curtain panel
- dressmaker's pins
- needle and thread

● Cut the ribbon into a number of lengths equal to the height of your sheer curtain plus 12.5cm (5in). Lay the ribbons on the curtain. At the top of the curtain, fold the ribbons over to form loops and pin them to the panel of sheer fabric. Make sure all the loops measure the same or the curtain won't hang straight.

● Sew through both thicknesses of ribbon and the curtain to secure the tab top. Repeat with all the ribbons right across the curtain.

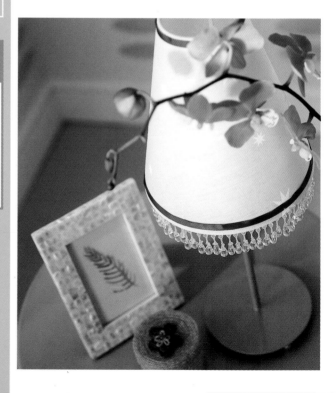

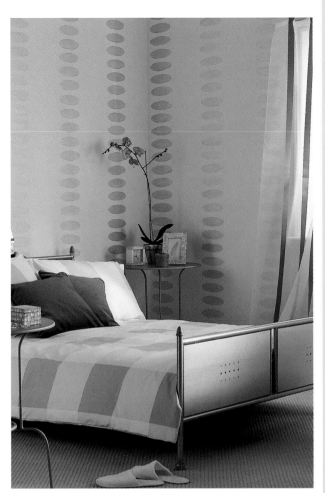

## Padded seat blanket box

- Paint the blanket box and let it dry. Cut the pink lamé to fit over the top of the piece of foam and tuck it underneath by 5cm (2in). Stick the fabric in place with foam glue, then stick the foam on to the box lid using foam glue.

- Place four lengths of ribbon across the pink lamé and staple them taut to the underside of the lid, turning under the raw ends of ribbon. Hot-glue the silver fringing around the edge of the lid of the box.

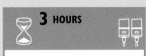

**3 HOURS**

**You will need**
- old blanket box
- oil-based paint in pale pink
- household paintbrush
- scissors and length of pink lamé
- tape measure
- 6–8.5cm (2½–3¼in) foam, cut to size of top of box
- foam glue
- lengths of pale pink ribbon
- staple gun and staples
- hot-glue gun
- silver fringing

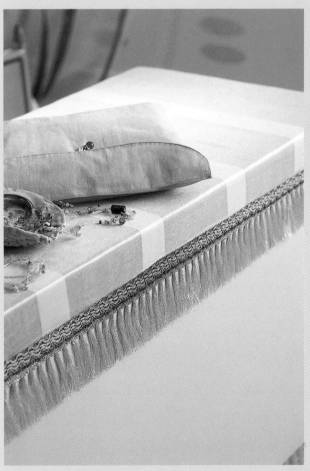

## Silver lozenge-stencilled wall

- First design your stencil shape – an oval shape was used here – on a piece of paper, then copy it on to stencil card. It will save you time if you repeat the motif across the card to create a line of ovals. Cut out the stencil using a craft knife.

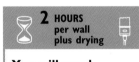

**2 HOURS**
**per wall**
**plus drying**

**You will need**
- pencil and paper
- stencil card and craft knife
- spray adhesive
- low-tack masking tape
- silver paint
- stencil brush
- tape measure

- Spray the back of the stencil with adhesive and stick it to the wall. Fix with masking tape and stencil with silver paint. Work out how far apart you want your columns of ovals and mark guidelines on the wall. Reposition the stencil and repeat painting.

# Springtime colours

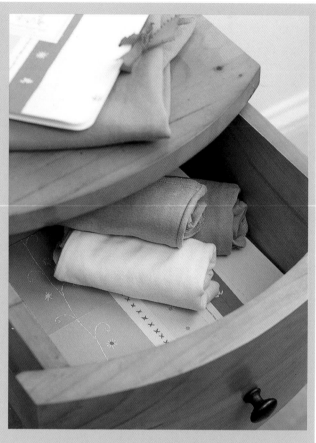

## Decorative fabric pelmet

• A fabric pelmet is ideal for enlivening a window with a plain roller blind. Cut a piece of fabric measuring slightly wider than your window and 15cm (6in) deep, plus an extra 2.5cm (1in) all round to allow for a hem. Hem the panel using iron-on tape. At evenly spaced intervals stitch loops of ribbon to the back of the panel from which to hang the panel from a curtain pole.

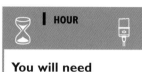

**⏳ I HOUR**

**You will need**
• scissors
• length of fabric
• tape measure
• iron-on no-sew tape
• short lengths of ribbon
• needle and thread

## Colourful drawer liner

• Press a sheet of newspaper into the bottom of the drawer to create an accurate template. Cut it out, then use the template to cut out a drawer liner to the correct size. Place it neatly in the bottom of the drawer.

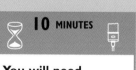

**⏳ I0 MINUTES**

**You will need**
• old newspaper
• scissors
• giftwrap

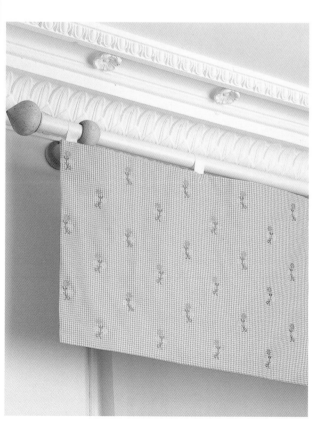

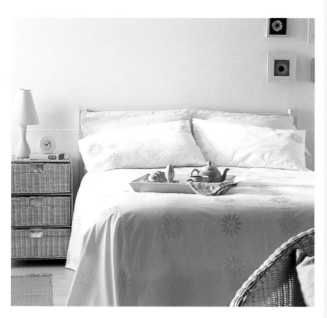

# Hand-painted gingham border

- Using a spirit level and a pencil, mark a horizontal line at dado rail height along the wall. Mask off either side to leave a 2cm (¾in) strip. Paint this stripe in green. Mark another line 10cm (4in) below the first, mask off as before and again paint green.

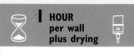

**HOUR**
per wall
plus drying

**You will need**
- spirit level and pencil
- tape measure
- low-tack masking tape
- emulsion paint in green and yellow
- household paintbrush
- set square

- When dry, mark vertical lines between these two green stripes at regular intervals to create squares – check that they are at right angles using a set square. Mask off and paint green. Halfway between the two green lines, mark a third horizontal line. Mask off and paint in yellow. Finally, add vertical lines in yellow to bisect the squares to create a gingham effect.

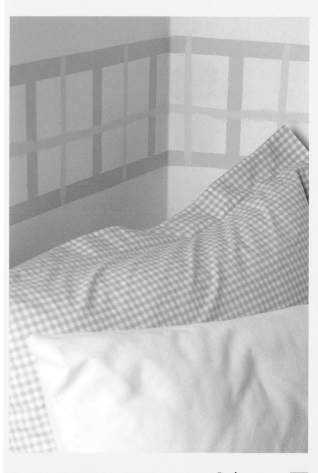

# Daisy-stamped bedlinen

- Pour the fabric paints on to the plates. Mix a touch of red into the yellow to get orange, and the yellow with a little green to make lime. Plan your pattern roughly on paper, then transfer it to your sheet or duvet, spread on to the floor.

**HOURS**
plus drying

**You will need**
- yellow, red and green fabric paints
- old plates for paint mixing
- pencil and paper
- plain bedding for stamping
- small roller with foam head
- daisy stamps, large and small
- clean cloth

- Coat the roller with paint, then roller paint on to a daisy stamp. Press the stamp firmly on to the sheet and hold for a couple of seconds. Re-coat with paint and repeat to produce the pattern you have planned. Leave to dry, then fix the paint by covering the design with a clean cloth and ironing on a hot setting.

# Lilac and silver tones

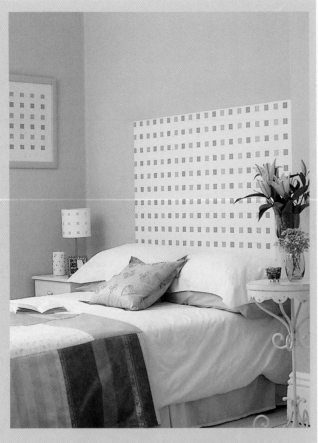

## Coordinate mismatched furniture

• Remove the old drawer handles, then cut the beading to fit the edges of the drawer fronts, using a mitre block for the corners. Paint the beading. When dry, use glue and panel pins to fit the beading to the front of the drawers. Paint the chest.

• When dry, measure the fronts of the drawers and cut the wallpaper to fit. Paste it on and smooth it flat. Touch up the paint if necessary and add new drawer knobs.

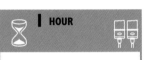

⏳ **1 HOUR**

**You will need**
- chest of drawers
- oil-based paint
- household paintbrush
- tape measure
- wallpaper scissors
- remnants of wallpaper
- wallpaper paste and brush
- handsaw and mitre block
- beading
- wood glue
- hammer and panel pins
- drawer knobs

## Wallpaper panel headboard

• Mark on the wall the size you want your headboard to be. Measure all the way down to the skirting board. Cut the wallpaper to size, paste and put it up on the wall. Smooth over with the wallpaper brush to ensure there are no air bubbles.

⏳ **45 MINUTES**

**You will need**
- pencil and tape measure
- wallpaper scissors
- wallpaper with geometric pattern
- wallpaper paste and brush

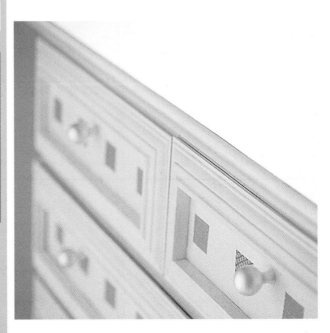

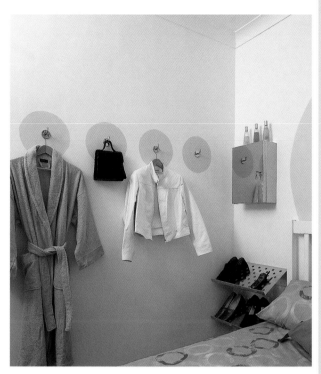

## Feature coat hooks

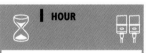

- Draw around a plate on to the stencil card and cut out the circle. Decide where you want your hooks to go, then tape the stencil card in place. Paint the circles where required. When dry, drill holes and screw a hook into the centre of each painted circle.

**⌛ I HOUR**

**You will need**
- plate, pencil and stencil card
- craft knife
- low-tack masking tape
- emulsion paint
- household paintbrush
- electric drill and wallplugs
- screwdriver and screws
- chrome coat hooks

## 'Frame' a plain mirror

- Mark a square on the wall at least 5cm (2in) wider and higher than the diameter of the mirror. Ensure it is level with a spirit level. Mask off and paint inside the square. Leave to dry, then hang your mirror in place.

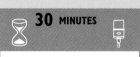

**⌛ 30 MINUTES**

**You will need**
- pencil and tape measure
- round mirror
- spirit level
- low-tack masking tape
- emulsion paint
- household paintbrush

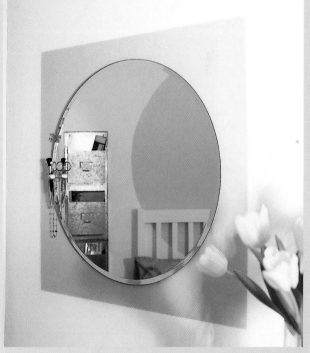

# Sorbet flavours

Introduce a touch of spring into your bedroom with storage ideas, bedroom furniture and knick-knacks in assorted sorbet colours.

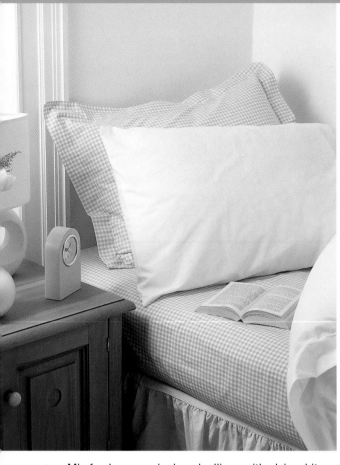

▲ Mix fresh green gingham bedlinen with plain white to create two sets of bedding with a whole new look.

▼ Use colourful sticky-backed plastic to cover old drawers for use as underbed storage.

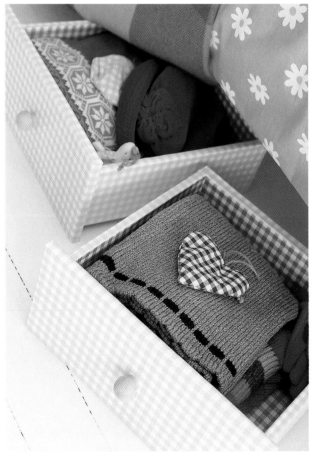

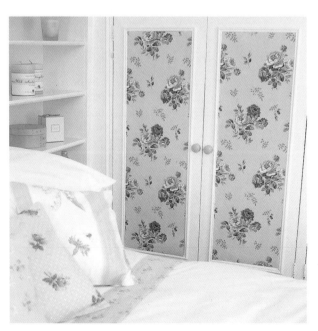

▲ Cut wallpaper to fit the panels of cupboard doors. Fix using wallpaper paste and finish with varnish.

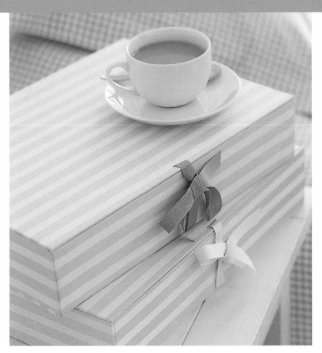

▲ Bedside reading can quickly turn into unruly piles of paper and books. Keep it all tidy in prettily striped, ribbon-tie boxes.

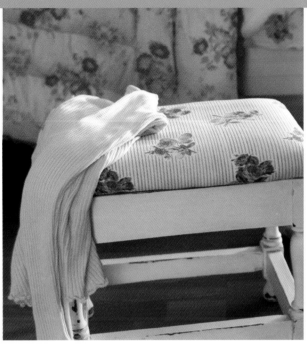

▲ Re-cover an old dressing table stool with fabric to match your room. Simply stretch it taut over the seat and fix in place using a staple gun.

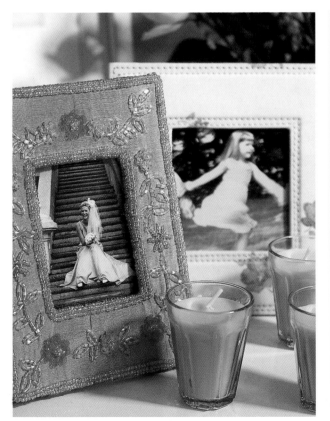

▲ Display family photos in glamorous frames around your bedroom to make you smile when you wake up.

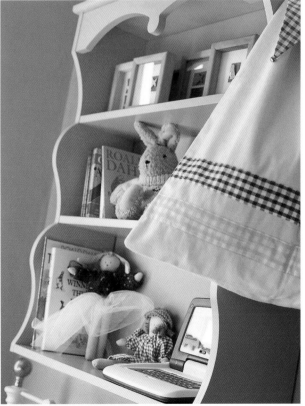

▲ Paint an old pine wall bookcase in a bright new colour. Use gloss paint for a good wipe-clean surface.

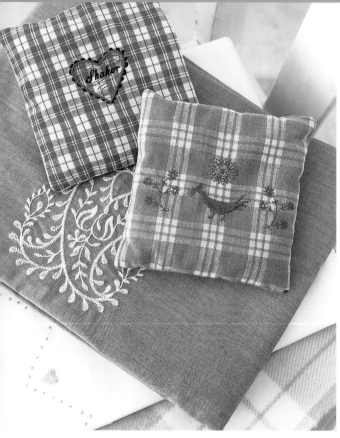

# Red, white and blue

Spruce up your bedroom with striking denim, red and white for a bright, fresh-looking colour scheme.

▲  Pile decorative cushions and pillows on the bed and on chairs for an inviting look of comfort.

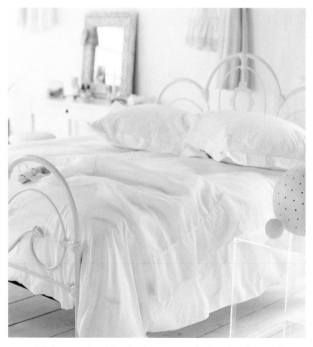

▲  Make an all-white bed a romantic focal point with layers of white-on-white bedding pillows and quilts.

▼  Give a cheap pine wardrobe an individual look by painting the front panels in toning stripes of blue.

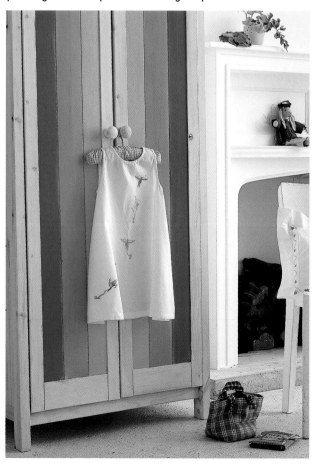

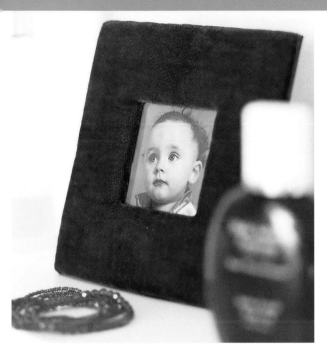

▲ Introduce a few shots of colour into an all-white bedroom with accessories like this sumptuous red velvet photo frame.

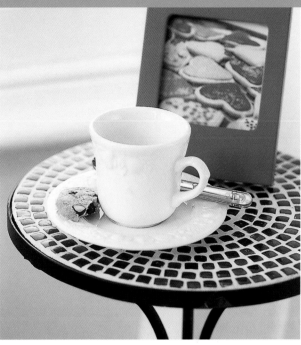

▲ Mosaic a table top to use as a bedside table. Spread the top with tile adhesive and press tiles individually into the adhesive to create a regular pattern.

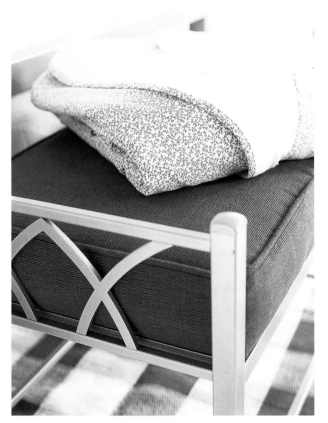

▲ Place a wide padded seat at the foot of the bed as somewhere to put clothes or to sit while getting dressed.

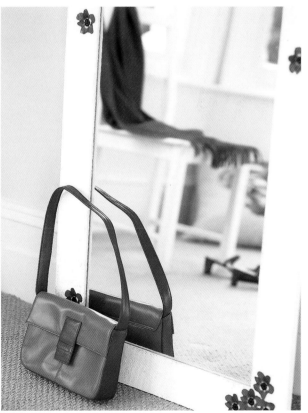

▲ Pretty up a mirror by painting the frame white and hand-painting simple floral designs around the edge.

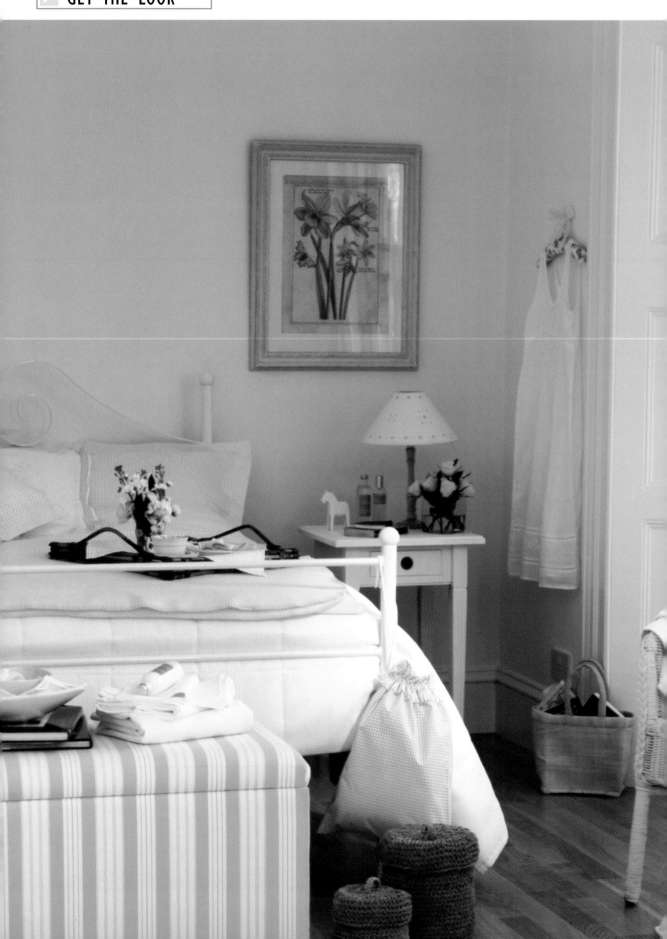

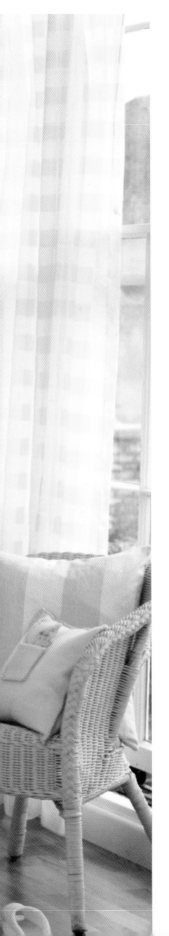

# Sunshine and light

**Combine buttercup yellow, white and warm wood for an uplifting bedroom.**

Yellow is the most energetic colour in the spectrum and the starting point for this room is the soft, rich shade on the walls, which is warm and bright without being overpowering. This is a room that will lift your spirits in the morning yet feel relaxed and comforting by lamplight.

Balance the yellow with plenty of fresh white on the woodwork, furniture and in the fabrics. Mix patterns – gingham on the bedlinen, stripes on the ottoman and checks at the window – to make sure the room feels comfortable rather than formal, and use sheer fabric at the window to make the most of light coming into the room.

The wooden floor, lampstand and picture frame are small but vital ingredients. Cherry and oak woods add just the right tone of warmth.

### What else would work?

• green and yellow stripes at the window
• seagrass flooring
• wallpaper with small floral motifs
• walnut or cherry bedstead

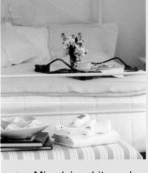

▲ Mix plain white and gingham bedlinen, add a soft yellow throw and trim a plain pillowcase with gingham ribbon.

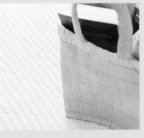

▲ Use a flat weave rug to add a bit of warmth and comfort underfoot.

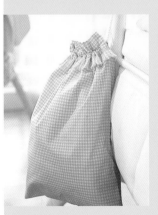

▲ Don't be afraid to mix checks, ginghams and stripes. Alternatively, use fabrics with plenty of texture instead, like raised cord or bobble weaves.

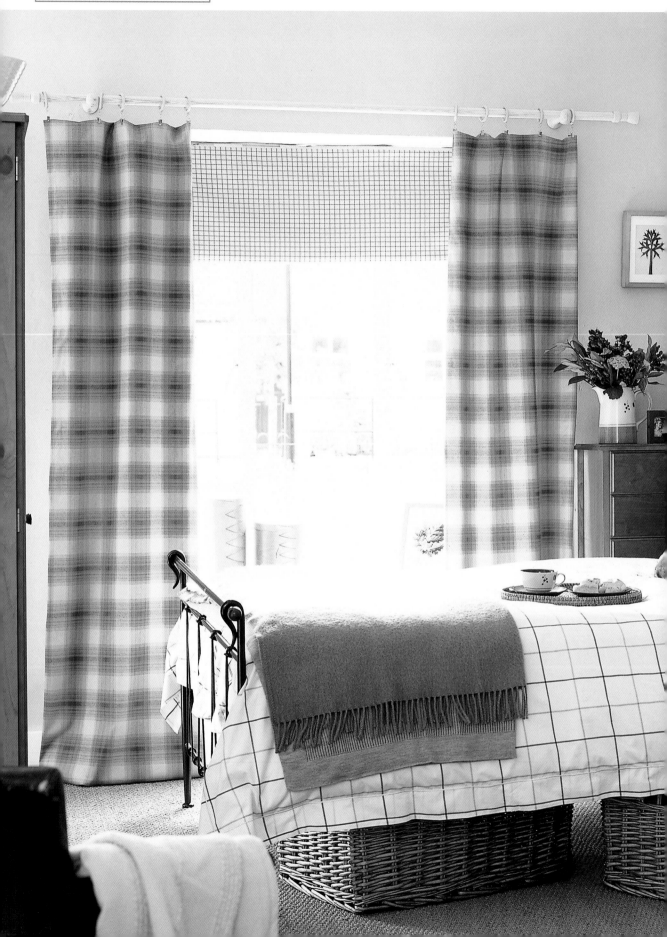

# Country cosiness

## Blend warm russet shades with soft greens to create easy country looks.

This is a country-style room to snuggle up in. Green and red are on opposite sides of the colour wheel, which means they work well together. If you don't want too strong a contrast, take your cue from this room and use muted shades. The soft sage strikes the right balance with the autumnal russet and the warm, glossy wood.

Be clever with texture to make the room feel really inviting. Layer the bed with pillows, felt and jersey throws. Have wicker baskets underneath the bed for country-style storage. The checked roller blind looks good and works well, but it is the blankets in place of curtains that bring a real feeling of warmth to the window. A coir carpet adds to the rustic texture in the room, but a ribbed runner beside the bed is gentler on bare feet.

### What else would work?

- oatmeal wool carpet
- sage green velvet curtains
- rust-coloured bedding
- leaf print voile at the window

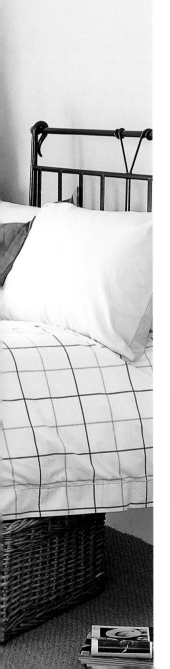

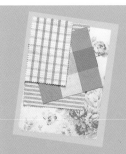

▲ Change the look completely for the warmer months by swapping the rust tartan curtains for lighter summery green checks or stripes.

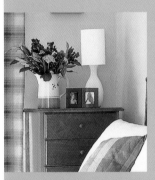

▲ Choose country-style accessories: wooden picture frames, cream lamps and a rustic jug used as a vase.

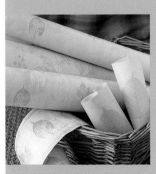

▲ Follow the autumnal theme through with leaf print wallpaper.

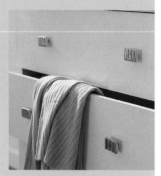

▲ Look for silver touches like vases, candlesticks, picture frames and beaded lampshades.

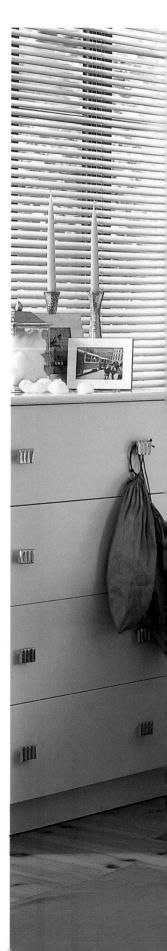

# Modern romantic look

## Let starry night skies inspire an atmospheric silver and deep lilac colour scheme.

Treat silver as the newest colour in your palette to create a bedroom that is contemporary yet romantic. The trick with silver is to use just touches rather than great swathes, so paint silver swirls on to pale walls, stamp blocks on to paper or look for wallpapers with shimmery motifs. Go for a plain white backdrop, then bring in deep lilac in the curtains, covered headboard and bed throw to add a touch of prettiness.

You could bring an extra dimension to the curtains by lining them with silver organza. The silver theme is delicately echoed in the star-spangled bedlinen, the drawer handles and the lamp and accessories.

To keep the look contemporary, choose clean lines and geometric shapes such as the bed, which is a modern take on the old-fashioned bedstead.

▲ Update an old chest of drawers by adding new, textured chrome handles.

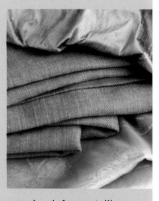

▲ Look for metallic fabrics such as silk dupions shot through with a hint of silver and shimmering organzas.

### What else would work?

• white, deep pile carpet
• raspberry pink instead of lilac
• sheers at the window
• pale beech flooring

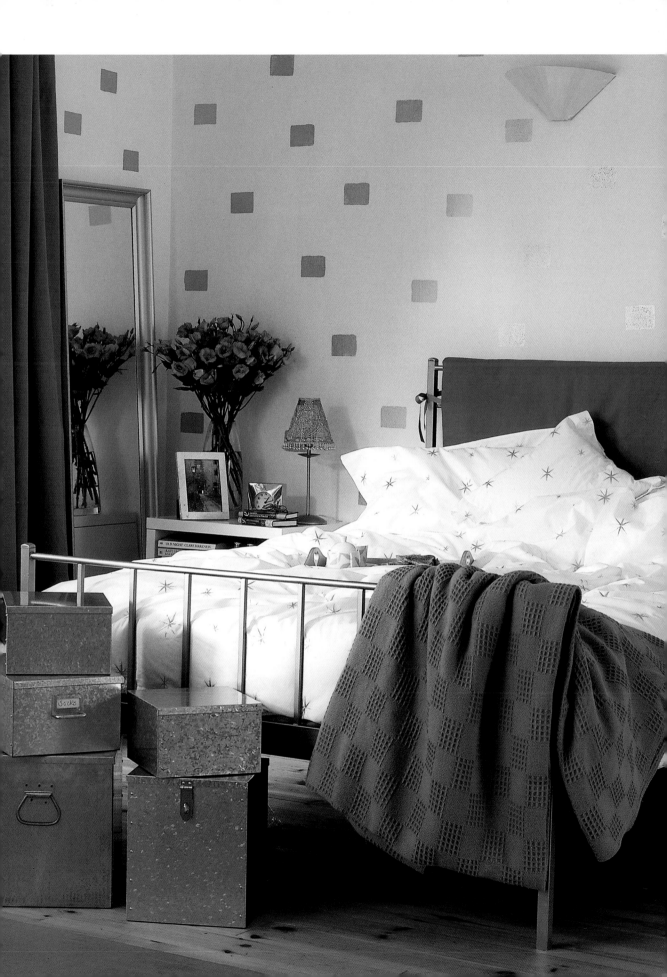

# Index

# Acknowledgements

All pictures copyright of The National Magazine Company Limited, except for the following listed below:

**Anaglypta/** (stockists tel: +44 (0) 1254 704 951) 69 right.
**Crown Paints/** www.crownpaint.co.uk
(reader advice line: +44 (0) 1254 704 951) 42 right, 68 left.
**Dulux/** www.dulux.co.uk (stockists tel: +44 (0) 1753 550 555) 58 bottom left, 74 bottom right, 76–77, 77 bottom right, 77 bottom centre.
**Elgin & Hall/** www.elgin.co.uk (stockists tel: +44 (0) 1677 450 100) 94 top left.
**Fired Earth/** www.firedearth.com (stockists tel: +44 (0) 1295 814 300) 72 bottom left.
**Octopus Publishing Group Limited** front cover bottom centre left, /Shona Wood back cover centre right.
**Ronseal/** www.ronseal.co.uk (stockists tel: +44 (0) 114 240 9469) 60.
**Samuel Heath & Sons PLC/** www.samuel-heath.com
(stockists tel: +44 (0) 121 766 4200) 95 top right.


**Executive Editor:** Anna Southgate
**Editor:** Rachel Lawrence
**Executive Art Editor:** Leigh Jones
**Designer:** Claire Harvey
**Picture Researcher:** Zoë Holtermann
***Your Home* Picture Coordination:** Jill Morgan
**Production Controller:** Louise Hall